550 Home Landscaping Ideas

550 Home

A ROUNDTABLE PRESS BOOK

CATRIONA T. ERLER AND DEREK FELL

PHOTOGRAPHS BY DEREK FELL

Landscaping Ideas

Simon and Schuster

NEW YORK LONDON TORONTO SYDNEY TOKYO

A ROUNDTABLE PRESS BOOK

Directors: Marsha Melnick and Susan E. Meyer
Project Editor: Melissa Schwarz
Editorial Assistant: Larry Dark
Design: Binns & Lubin / Betty Binns
Color Separations: Oceanic Graphic Printing, Inc.

SIMON AND SCHUSTER
Simon & Schuster Building
Rockefeller Center
1230 Avenue of the Americas
New York, N.Y. 10020

SIMON AND SCHUSTER and colophon are registered trademarks
of Simon & Schuster Inc.

Printed and bound in Hong Kong

10 9 8 7 6 5 4 3 2

Library of Congress Cataloging-in-Publication Data

Erler, Catriona T.
550 home landscaping ideas / Catriona T. Erler and Derek Fell;
photographs by Derek Fell.
    p.   cm.
"A Roundtable Press book"—T.p. verso
ISBN 0-671-74429-1
1. Landscape gardening. 2. Gardens—Styles. 3. Gardens—
Designs and plans. 4. Gardens—Pictorial works. I. Fell, Derek
II. Title. III. Title: Five hundred fifty home landscaping ideas.
SB473.E75 1991   91-17812
  712'.6—dc20   CIP
                  r91

Acknowledgments

Catriona Tudor Erler would like to express her appreciation to her family for their encouragement and patience while this book was being written.

Derek Fell wishes to thank the following landscape architects and garden designers for permission to photograph their garden designs:

Brickman Industries, Langhorne, Pennsylvania

Kurt Bluemel, Baldwin, Maryland

Creative Landscaping, East Hampton, New York

Robert Fletcher, Pacific Palisades, California

John Greelee, Pomona, California

John Harlow, Tucson, Arizona

Hiroshi Makita, Collegeville, Pennsylvania

Dennis Shaw, Santa Barbara, California

Oehme, van Sweden & Associates, Washington, DC

Plimpton Associates, Ormond Beach, Florida

Carter van Dyke, Doylestown, Pennsylvania

Also, thanks to Kathy Nelson and Wendy Fields who help manage the horticultural picture library at Cedaridge Farm, Pennsylvania.

Contents

Chapter Five: Garden Habitats   *144*

Chapter Six: Color Theme Gardens   *170*

Chapter Seven: Seasonal Gardens   *178*

Index, 189

Introduction

DESIGNING A GARDEN that truly suits your personality and needs calls for thoughtful attention and a seemingly endless flow of ideas. This book was written to fuel those ideas and to help promote creative problem solving. Though it does not teach the basic principles of landscape design (which are readily available elsewhere), these principles appear again and again in different contexts, and you will certainly absorb them if you read the book from cover to cover. It was our intention that this book be used primarily as a source of inspiration, and it has been designed and organized toward that end. There are eighty-one sections on garden design topics. However, it also pays to look beyond the specific topic that seems to most closely fit your current needs. For example, if you are planning a Japanese-style garden, or simply want to add an Oriental flavor to your present design, study the Japanese section for an overview, but also refer to other sections. Review the sections on related plant themes such as irises, ornamental grasses, and trees or appropriate accents like waterfalls, paths and avenues, and bridges; the section on your own region; and the chapter on seasonal gardens.

To select the 550 ideas in the book, we studied and discussed literally thousands of color photographs, taken over a period of 15 years. Ultimately, we chose those that best illustrate popular landscaping concepts and demonstrate a strong sense of design and an imaginative use of either plants (softscape) or structures (hardscape), or a pleasing combination of the two. Examples were selected because they are classic (such as the quadrant herb garden at the historic Peter Wentz Farmstead, near Philadelphia, where General George Washington slept during his Valley Forge campaign—on page 18) or innovative (including the easy-maintenance ornamental grass garden

and informal swimming pool of nurseryman Kurt Bluemel, a pioneer in ornamental grass gardening in North America—on page 9). Some were designed by landscape professionals, some by talented property owners; others are the result of a close collaboration between the two.

The ideas themselves range in size from full-scale designs to charming details. While many can be copied exactly (Claude Monet's bench, for example, on page 101), the intent is for you to adapt and even improve them. Some of the ideas are simple, others are challenging, but all are useful in a North American "home landscape." Anything too grand or pretentious was rejected. Ideas for English parkscapes, Scottish manors, and French chateaux abound in countless books extolling the beauty of properties from a bygone age, but they offer little of practical value to a gardener who must work with a different plant palette and different construction materials, within wholly dissimilar climate and size constraints.

Before embarking on a landscaping project, you must make several decisions based on your lifestyle, your budget, and your own style preferences. In addition, you must decide whether you want to do the work yourself or hire someone to help you with the design.

Lifestyle

Be sure that your garden is designed to suit the way you live. For example, if you enjoy entertaining in the garden, allow ample space for guests, as well as for tables and chairs. Remember that children (your own or those of your guests) need play space. If you live in a warm climate and spend a lot of time outside, create furnished garden living rooms, rather than a design

Decide how much interest you have in the garden and how much time you want to devote to its design and maintenance. Gardens that rely on evergreen ground covers and hardscape can look beautiful and require only a minimum amount of care. On the other hand, a garden that contains lots of flower beds and fast-growing plants that need pruning requires extensive regular upkeep. Of course, it is possible to cheat on maintenance: if the design you prefer requires lots of work, but your free time is limited, substitute less demanding plants to achieve a sophisticated look that doesn't require as much care.

Money Matters

Even a small suburban lot can cost more than a hundred thousand dollars to landscape if the design includes a swimming pool, a lot of hardscape, expensive specimen plants, and a landscape architect's fees. On the other hand, if you do much of the work yourself, start with small plants, grow scarce plants from seed, and keep the design simple, you can create a charming garden for relatively little money.

Start with a master plan that's affordable, then develop it as your budget allows. Don't scrimp on essentials, such as good soil or adequate irrigation. Although these may not be as emotionally satisfying or as dramatic as a beautiful plant or structure, they are critical to the success of the whole scheme. If you are starting from scratch, have a thorough soil analysis done, and consider the water demands of your garden to determine whether it can be watered by hand during dry spells or will need a more reliable irrigation system.

Remember, watering also adds to the expense of your garden. In regions of the country where water shortage is an issue and municipalities may impose a ban on watering during periods of drought, plan a garden of drought-tolerant native plants. Fortunately, using plants that are water-misers does not mean sacrificing beauty. The diversity of available plants is increasing yearly as nurseries respond to the demands of their clientele by studying xeriscaping (landscaping for drought tolerance).

Keep in mind that a specific look can often be achieved by less expensive means. A brick terrace, for example, can be costly, but flagstone may be a good substitute. Grass is even less expensive than stone if you plant it yourself, but upkeep costs will be greater. No matter what your budget is, it pays to consider all options carefully.

Choosing a Landscape Designer or Architect

If you decide to enlist professional help in designing your garden, you need to choose between a landscape designer and a landscape architect. Landscape designers are knowledgeable about plant materials and design principles, but may not have any formal training; landscape architects have a degree in engineering as well as horticultural and design experience. As a rule, if your plan includes hardscaping structures—from walls, pools, and ponds, to gazebos, pool houses, and storage sheds—you will probably need a landscape architect, as well as a landscape contractor to implement the architect's plans.

When choosing either type of professional, ask around for recommendations, then look at portfolios. When you find someone you like, ask for references from former clients. Find out if the designer or architect came in on budget, kept to the agreed-upon schedule, and was flexible and willing to listen to

the client's needs and desires. Also ask to see the gardens the person you're considering designed. This is important because photographs can enlarge or diminish the space or hide an undesirable feature.

If you have trouble finding the right person, consider enrolling in a landscape design course. Classes are often a good way to get referrals for people who are well respected in the field, and in the process you will learn a lot that will help you guide a professional to meet your needs.

When you are ready to make a choice, consider whether your landscape designer or architect is someone you can work with comfortably. You will be much happier if you feel actively involved in the design process. In general, the best home landscapes are produced when there is some active participation by the owner. Avoid anyone who doesn't welcome your participation, and be wary of someone whose personality doesn't seem to mesh with yours. You will be spending a lot of time together making decisions, so choose a professional who sparks your creativity and will listen to your ideas.

In the end, you and the designer or architect may both need to make compromises. One satisfied client described his experi-

ence this way: "We have a contemporary house. Our landscape architect thought the garden design should be simple and manicured to fit the house. I was used to a more natural, traditional look, so he incorporated more natural flower beds at the edge of the property. I also wanted lots of trees and shrubs in the back, but our architect pointed out that they would soon block our view of the ocean. I learned a lot from him—he was a wonderful teacher."

The landscape architect on the same project was also willing to make concessions. "The trees the client wanted near the driveway were not really suitable because they have very invasive roots," he said. "But the customer really wanted them, so we built 4-foot-deep concrete cells around the trees to keep the roots from spreading under the driveway."

Planning the Garden

Whether you are working with a professional or on your own, it is important to do your homework. Use books as references, and mark the styles and ideas that either strike a chord in you or deal with a situation that applies to your own garden. Look through magazines that feature outstanding gardens as well, and mark the ones you like. You will probably notice a pattern in your choices—specific plants, garden features, and design styles—that will help clarify what you want to achieve. If you are working with a landscape designer or architect, having a collection of photos to discuss will also help communicate what you want.

When looking at photographs of other gardens, bear in mind that an idea implemented on a grand scale can often be reduced to work in a much smaller area. Don't disregard a design you like just because it's planted on acres and you have only a few square feet. A good designer can help you create visual illusions in your garden to make a small space feel bigger or an impersonal area feel more intimate.

Having a garden is an ongoing process. Even after you have your basic garden design, keep searching for ideas as you continue to make additions and changes. As H. E. Bates said in his book *A Love of Flowers,* "A garden that is finished is dead. A garden should be in a constant state of fluid change, expansion, experiment, adventure; above all it should be an inquisitive, loving, but self-critical journey on the part of the owner."

International Gardens

HUMAN BEINGS HAVE cultivated gardens as a means of food from the time they discovered that seeds grow into plants. But the idea of planting a garden for purely decorative purposes developed much more recently. Historians are unsure precisely when the first ornamental gardens were planted, but most agree that the Chinese and the Romans were among the first to perfect the idea, probably more than 2,500 years ago.

Ever since then, ornamental gardening has flourished throughout the world, especially during periods of prosperity. Each country has put its own unique stamp on garden design. Today, we often identify distinct garden styles as being typical of a nation or a period in a particular nation's history. Each reflects the climate, topography, and culture of that country, and often emotional, spiritual, and political values as well.

In many cases an especially successful garden design concept was borrowed from one country and absorbed into the traditions of another. Parterres, which we generally think of as French, originated in Italy. Chinese garden design, which originated in monasteries designed for meditation and contemplation, greatly influenced Japanese garden design

Perhaps due to North America's rich ethnic mix, Americans and Canadians are particularly adept at taking design ideas from abroad and adapting them. The variety in climate and topography found throughout North America makes it possible for Americans to consider garden styles from all over the world, sometimes even incorporating many themes into a single garden—like a horticultural Disney World.

American Colonial Gardens

This section includes American Colonial gardens simply because they are from a time past and therefore foreign to us today.

Most colonists in the eighteenth century cultivated the plants they were familiar with, those they had brought from "back home" in Europe. In some cases this was successful; however, because of the different climate, many imports—such as sweet peas and fuchsias—tended to fail, except in isolated microclimates.

The earliest Colonial gardens featured herbs arranged in "quadrants"—four square beds, intersected by paths, surrounded by a rectangular border and enclosed by a fence. Annual herbs and vegetables were planted in the squares, while perennial herbs and berry bushes grew in the border, inside the fence. These gardens were generally located close to the kitchen door since many of the herbs, such as rosemary and parsley, were used in cooking, while others, such as lavender and chamomile, were used to mask household odors. Medicinal plants—mint to clear sinuses, rhubarb as a purgative—and dye plants, such as dyer's woad, were also planted, in clumps or short rows. A few ornamental plants—especially cottage pinks (Dianthus), hollyhocks, and shrub roses, all popular in English cottage gardens—were sometimes added just inside the fence.

In time, the wealthier colonists wanted more sophisticated gardens. In 1710, when Lieutenant Governor Alexander Spotswood arrived in Williamsburg, Virginia, to assume his responsibility as a representative of the British Crown, he had been accustomed to discussing business while strolling among well-tended private gardens; he felt his station in Britain's largest American colony deserved similar gracious living. However, he caused much resentment among the local townspeople when he used their taxes to plant an elaborate formal garden featuring terraced lawns, boxwood parterres, espaliered fruit trees, pleached beech allées, and a large free-form water garden overhung with weeping birch and southern live oak trees. Brick paths and corridors formed by high holly hedges led visitors from one garden room to another, and a high red brick wall enclosed the entire landscaped area.

With Spotswood's estate serving as example, Williamsburg soon became well known for its charming town gardens. Writing to a friend about the beautiful coastal city of Annapolis, Maryland, Thomas Jefferson once said that while the architecture there was generally better than in Williamsburg, the gardens were not.

Over the next hundred years, whether planted with European imports or local flora, American Colonial gardens were generally very well-ordered places. Products of the Age of Reason, Colonial gardeners preferred symmetrical designs with brick paths, ornate wooden fences, and paired elements such as ornaments and benches, creating a definite sense of balance and control over the wilderness. Even major specimen plants were often arranged in balanced pairs or groups of four.

By the early nineteenth century the colonists were well established in their newly formed country. The innovative gardeners among them fell under the influence of the maverick English landscape designer Lancelot "Capability" Brown. Brown's style was a departure from formal design, toward more naturalized landscapes, highlighted by sweeping vistas. Horticulturally, it marked the end of the Colonial era in America.

Chinese Gardens

A Chinese garden is a complex blend of elements designed to make the garden experience not only emotionally and visually satisfying, but spiritually uplifting as well. Today, a distinct Chinese-style garden design is not as familiar to Americans as a Japanese one. Yet the Chinese were among the first to interpret nature's beauty in a garden setting and had already developed a highly sophisticated style as early as A.D. 1370. Chinese ideas strongly influenced the Japanese. Even bonsai, which we generally associate with Japan, came out of China. The Chinese took miniature trees from the wild that had been stunted by wind, salt spray, or rocky soil and planted them in their gardens. Later the Japanese put a new twist on the art by purposefully growing dwarf trees in shallow containers, pruning their roots and branches. The word "bonsai" translates literally as "planted in a tray."

Miniaturized trees are in fact a symbol of Chinese gardens. In general, the Chinese approach to landscape design is to reproduce a lofty, majestic mountain scene by scaling it down to garden size. Beautiful rocks with jagged forms are brought into the garden from the surrounding countryside and arranged to look like upthrusting mountains. Other stones, chosen because they resemble an animal or bird, are positioned like sculptures and given names.

Chinese gardens are typically enclosed, creating a private domain removed from the chaos and clutter of the outside world. Within this secluded space, they are designed to perfect nature's beauty. Walls, fences, and hedges surround the gardens, but whenever possible, the topography of the land itself is used to enhance the sense of privacy, creating a cup garden. On a large scale, a cup garden might include the hillsides surrounding a central lake, for a beautiful bowl-like feeling. Paths around the lake and up and down hills lead visitors to unexpected pleasures: a new perspective on a vista, the melodious play of water

over rocks, or an especially exquisite delicate plant. But even a tiny Chinese garden can have a cup element, an intimate spot that draws the viewer's attention to one special feature, perhaps a plant, a rock sculpture, or a small pond.

English Gardens

As a nation of gardeners, the English have perfected several distinct garden styles over the centuries. In the eighteenth century a trend known as the English landscape movement began to break away from borrowed French conventions—huge formal compositions based on straight avenues and geometric basins that extended the axis of the house. Instead, the new gardens had a more natural look typified by great country houses set in rolling park land. The concept reached its peak in the second half of the century with the work of designers such as Capability Brown, who created idealized, natural-looking landscapes with sloping lawns and groves of trees, taking care to tie in the garden visually to the untamed landscape beyond its precincts.

By the Victorian age the rise of the British middle class made gardening accessible to more people. Inventions such as the lawn mower and the rubber hose (which replaced a leather hose) made it possible to maintain a property without an army of gardeners. The Victorian era was also the heyday of British plant collecting. Intrepid explorers rambled the entire British Empire collecting plants and brought them home to England. The new breed of garden enthusiasts then planted theme gardens featuring a particular genus or plant family, such as rhododendrons, ferns, roses, or heathers. Those who didn't collect generally planted a typical Victorian garden characterized by a series of beds in which showy plants were grouped en masse, a process called bedding-out or carpet bedding (see page 45).

In the early twentieth century an Edwardian woman named Gertrude Jekyll again revolutionized English gardening. Rebelling against what she called the "ingenious monstrosity" of carpet bedding, she and her colleague William Robinson popularized the concept of a perennial border with plants mixed in a way that highlighted their lovely colors and forms (see page 42). These borders were essentially a refinement of the charming, unsophisticated cottage gardens that Jekyll admired, and they had already caused a sensation in some Scottish estate gardens.

Collaborating with Sir Edwin Lutyens, an architect, Jekyll designed more than 200 gardens, making such an important mark on English garden design that her style is now considered typically English, and many of her books on garden philosophy have been reprinted. In her book *Visions of Paradise,* Susan Littlefield summarized the style Jekyll and Lutyens developed as a garden "structured tightly around a framework of walls, hedges, beds, borders, and paved pathways. These are the garden's bones, and whether built of stone or made of plants, they create its scale, order, and coherence. If the flowers and shrubs bloom profusely and if the planting is particularly choice, the result will

be a truly English garden—formally planned but informally planted."

Victoria (Vita) Sackville-West, who with her husband, Harold Nicolson, created the garden at their home, Sissinghurst Castle, described their design similarly, calling it "the strictest formality of design combined with a strict informality in planting."

French Gardens

French garden design, still known for its elegance, reached its peak of ostentation and splendor in the late seventeenth century, under the reign of Louis XIV. A French nobleman's garden had to reflect his power and authority, and the king's garden at the Palace of Versailles was the most glorious of all. It is said that Louis XIV imprisoned his minister of finance, Nicholas Fouquet, claiming that Fouquet's house and garden at Vaux-le-Vicomte were so elaborate they could only have been financed with government funds. The king then commanded Fouquet's landscape architect, André Le Nôtre, to design an even more grandiose residence and garden at Versailles.

Inspired by Italian Renaissance designs, landscape designers like Le Nôtre adapted elements of grand, terraced hillside gardens in Italy to fit the flat landscape around Paris. Determined to outdo their mentors, French royal gardeners found ways to make these garden features more and more monumental: wide avenues stretching to the horizon, rectangular canals large enough to float boats, gilt waterworks such as the Fountain of Apollo at Versailles, and large grottoes and temples tucked away in thickets called "boskets" became the norm. Boxwood parteres were planted in more elaborate patterns than had ever been attempted in Italy and were then filled with seasonal flowers.

Based on the geometric principles introduced by the seventeenth century French philosopher and mathematician René Descartes, the garden elements were organized around a central axis. Beds and paths were symmetrical, and ornaments such as statues and urns were usually displayed in pairs or sets of four. Plants were treated as architectural features—pruned into geometric shapes and placed in rows to create allées or to line canals.

In North America just prior to the Depression, it became fashionable among wealthy industrialists to emulate the gardens of Versailles. Though some of these gardens have fallen into neglect due to lack of funds, many good examples remain—the Biltmore House and Garden in North Carolina, Old Westbury Garden in New York, and Nemours Mansion in Delaware.

In recent years another garden style has become popular in France and subsequently in America: the "Normandy" garden, exemplified by the garden designed by Claude Monet when he settled in the village of Giverny, north of Paris. Normandy gardens are essentially cottage gardens filled with flowers. They feature plants spilling into paths, vines scrambling up walls, and roses trained over rustic arbors, with tall-growing plants such as dahlias, hollyhocks, and sunflowers carrying color high into the sky. The artists Pierre-Auguste Renoir and Vincent van Gogh, like Monet, found many favorite subjects to paint in this kind of garden.

Italian Gardens

To escape the heat of summer in the cities, wealthy Italians during the Renaissance period retreated to the country, where they built splendid hilltop villas and enjoyed panoramic views and cooling breezes. The gardens built around these villas were extensions of the home—terraced "rooms" cut into the slope, overlooking the plains below. These are what we think of today as the quintessential Italian garden.

Typically, garden rooms closest to the house were the most formal, with precisely clipped shrubs arranged in simple but striking geometric designs. A blend of green foliage created a rich tapestry against which a few flowering plants—often varied types in different shades of one color—were displayed. Statuary, columns, stone balustrades, and urns furnished these rooms, their white Carrara marble standing out beautifully against the dark green foliage. Stone staircases, some extremely grand, connected the different levels, with the terraces becoming greener, shadier, and less formal farther from the house.

Further taking advantage of their hillsides, sixteenth-century Italians developed elaborate waterworks, with watercourses that flowed through the many garden levels, adding a cooling musical element as well as a lively focus to the design. Most famous is the Villa d'Este with hundreds of different fountains, channels, and falls demonstrating the limitless ways water can flow. In many gardens a cool grotto, where people can retreat from the hot sun, interrupts a stream of water.

The influence of Italian gardens is widespread. Their classic geometric designs were the inspiration for seventeenth-century French gardens. The concept also traveled to England and North America. As recently as the 1950s, landscape designer Thomas Church made his mark by adapting the Italian garden idea of outdoor living space to California, making Italianate garden rooms an indispensable feature of the California lifestyle.

Japanese Gardens

There is a distinctive look to a Japanese garden that is easy to recognize but difficult to duplicate. According to premier Japanese landscape designers, it takes a lifetime to master the art. Even the seemingly most simple designs are a complex blend of symbols imbued with the spirit of Zen Buddhism.

There are three important elements in a Japanese landscape design. Water, a universal symbol of life, is almost always present. Even a dry garden often suggests water with a pebble stream or with sand raked in patterns to represent ripples or waves. Stones play an important role as well and are often

assigned special meanings, such as the Guardian Stone, Moon Stone (for solitude), Worship Stone, Stone of Easy Rest, and Shoe-Removing Stone. The way these stones are placed in relation to one another communicates special meanings, too. Trees are the third important element in a Japanese garden—especially evergreens. Generally three-quarters of the woody plants (trees and shrubs) in a Japanese garden are evergreen, with deciduous trees chosen mostly to provide springtime blossoms (cherry trees) or spectacular fall foliage (ginkos or maples).

Although color is an important element in Japanese gardens, floral color is a relatively minor feature, often representing less than 20 percent of the garden and usually introduced as a mass planting of one variety, such as a sweep of Japanese irises. Instead, the Japanese plant for a variety of leaf forms and textures, as well as shades of green. Japanese maples, which come in a wide choice of leaf colors and forms, are especially prized, along with various pines. Evergreen azaleas and camellias are also appreciated and are often artistically shaped into visually soothing mounds.

The Japanese garden style most favored by Westerners is the *Tsuki-yama,* meaning "high lands," where variety and interest are most obvious. Built on multiple levels, rather than on flat ground, these are adventurous stroll gardens with paths leading over bridges and along ridges. On the way the visitor will encounter contemplative scenes, such as a lantern placed on a mossy rock or a pattern of fallen leaves on an earth mound, as well as pagodas, teahouses, and vast vistas across ponds or through trees.

Japanese-style gardens can be adapted to almost any climate. They are a welcome respite for busy Westerners, who appreciate their serenity and sense of order over chaos.

Spanish Gardens

The first European gardens in North America were Spanish-style Mission gardens planted in Florida and the Southwest in the sixteenth century by settlers from Spain. During the eighteenth century Father Junipero Serra and the Franciscan monks established twenty-nine missions between San Diego and San Francisco, a day's journey apart. Each had an enclosed garden. As Spanish colonists followed the missionaries, they too built courtyard gardens featuring grillwork, colorful tiles, and a fountain or well as a focal point.

Interest in the Spanish garden style waned some during the nineteenth century, but when beautiful Spanish gardens were put on display at the Pan American Exposition in San Diego in 1915, they became more popular once again. Spanish- or Mediterranean-style architecture and garden design have flourished in the Southwest and Florida ever since.

Although similar in structure to Italian gardens, Spanish gardens are more colorful and include a wider variety of sweet-scented plants—especially jasmine and citrus. The bougainvillea vine is almost a trademark of Spanish gardens, as are olive trees, the cork oak, and the Canary Island date palm. Calla lilies are frequently planted in pots and angel's trumpets in tubs. Brightly painted glazed tiles are used prolifically, decorating fountains, benches, walls, and even stair risers (see page 132).

Since Spanish colonists were highly religious, their gardens often feature a religious scene—perhaps a statue of the Madonna recessed into a wall or a sequence of tiles depicting scenes from the Bible. Archways, with potted plants clustered around the uprights and climbing banksia roses growing in narrow beds along walls, are other common embellishments.

Carmel Mission in California has one of the best examples of a Spanish garden. At Longue Vue Gardens in New Orleans, a Spanish-style garden features a large rectangular pool rimmed with plants in terra-cotta pots and a long, narrow water channel similar to one found in the famous gardens at the Alhambra Palace in Granada, Spain.

Throughout history people have been inspired by garden design ideas from different countries and eras, adapting them to their own tastes and trends. By combining and modifying garden styles from around the world and throughout time you can make your own unique statement.

▶

Influenced by eighteenth-century rationalism, Colonial gardeners designed their garden beds in simple geometric patterns. John Bartram's historic garden on the banks of the Schuylkill River in Philadelphia is a fine example of the Colonial penchant for simplicity. The outside flower border has been carefully aligned with the house, and the inner square bed is centered exactly.

Bartram founded the first botanical garden in America in 1728 and was one of the earliest botanists to collect plants from the wild. His collection of native plants was considered the finest in the country. George Washington and Thomas Jefferson, both avid gardeners, often called on him for horticultural advice.

▼

In Colonial gardens, such elements as ornaments, benches, garden beds, and plants were generally used in pairs to create a sense of symmetry and balance. Here a millstone and a stone horse trough, two durable relics of Colonial life, were paired to evoke the era in a modern garden.

◄

Plant a Colonial-style garden using old-fashioned plant species instead of modern hybrids. Generally, early species have small, single flowers and leggy stems. Growing in this historic garden at Old Sturbridge Village, Massachusetts, are impatiens, balsam, yellow annual coreopsis, summer phlox, and, in the back, magenta four-o'clocks.

◄ Create a formal Colonial garden with symmetrical beds outlined with boxwood parterres. An elaborate Chippendale-style gazebo and connecting trellis arbor dramatically increase the sense of elegance and formality.

▼ A quadrant garden is a favorite Colonial motif for both flowers and vegetables. Here at the Peter Wentz Farmstead in Pennsylvania, a path cuts both ways through the center of the vegetable garden, dividing it into four equal squares. The entire plot is enclosed with a rustic wooden fence to define the area and keep out stray animals.

▲ Living in an era without air-conditioning, Colonial gardeners planted "ghost tunnels" as cool places to walk in the garden—or as private retreats. This tunnel at the Governor's Palace in Williamsburg, Virginia, is made with parallel rows of beech trees woven together at the top. The weaving technique is known as pleaching.

► A Colonial-style garden shed will add an immediate sense of the era to your garden. This cylindrical building at the historic Highlands garden near Philadelphia was probably originally an outhouse. Notice the way the sun shines through the pink-saucer magnolia blossoms *(Magnolia × Soulangiana)*, creating a "lace curtain" screen in front of the building.

A Chinese-style structure is always an effective way to give a Chinese feeling to a garden. This Chinese pagoda in the Dr. Sun Yat-sen garden in Vancouver, British Columbia, is the most famous in North America. The garden embodies the essence of Chinese garden design: a miniature mountain panorama that highlights fascinating rocks and is complete with paths to stroll and goals to head toward, such as the pagoda on top of the hill.

The Chinese decorate their gardens not only with sculpture but also with rocks that have fascinating shapes or forms resembling animals. The stones are given names such as "dragon rock" or "owl rock."

To create the scaled-down mountain scenes so admired by Chinese landscape designers, use rocks in their natural form. Here a natural cup or channel in a rock becomes a flume through which water can flow. The stone retaining wall looks like a rocky cliff. Lotuses *(Nelumbo)* are particularly loved by the Chinese for their umbrella-shaped leaves and large, marble-sized seeds, which can live for thousands of years.

Evoke a sense of China by using a dragon sculpture as a garden accent. In Chinese mythology, the dragon is an important character, viewed as a god and used as a royal emblem. A dragon would be out of place in a Japanese garden since it was never popular in Japanese folk stories.

The Chinese enjoy miniaturized trees and plants, like Japanese bonsai, and were the first to recognize the ornamental value of growing dwarfed trees in their gardens. However, instead of limiting growth by keeping a plant root-bound in a container, the Chinese prefer a more naturalized setting, such as a crevice in a rock. Here columbine plants *(Aquilegia)* eke out their existence in the crannies of stacked stones.

The Chinese are fascinated by mountain landscapes and copy them on a smaller scale. Most are "stroll gardens" with paths leading up hill and down dale, opening to new vistas and stopping for intimate moments in tiny cup gardens set within the larger surroundings. Inspired by this Chinese tradition, Walter Beck designed the Innisfree garden at his home near Millbrook, New York, to resemble a mountain panorama.

A classic English cottage garden, such as this one planted by Vita Sackville-West at Sissinghurst, in England, is a charming jumble of edible and ornamental plants intermixed so densely that weeds don't stand a chance. Generally the space is contained, bordered on one side by the house or cottage and on the other three by walls, hedges, or fences, all of which are covered with vining plants. A path leads from the garden gate to the front door of the house.

English cottage gardens are small, intimate places packed with a remarkably diverse collection of plants, many of old-fashioned varieties. Classic plants for a cottage garden include white lilies, clove-scented pinks *(Dianthus)*, honeysuckle, roses, primroses, lavender, hollyhocks, hawthorns, amaranthus, and mignonettes.

The herbaceous border is a trademark of Englishness in a garden. It was first popularized by English garden writer William Robinson in his book *The English Flower Garden* (1883). The concept was perfected by Gertrude Jekyll, a turn-of-the-century English plantswoman who rebelled against the then-prevailing system of mass planting annuals for summer.

Ideally an herbaceous border should face south with a wall or dark hedge behind it and a path of stone or grass in front of it. The goal—and challenge—is to mix annuals and perennials to achieve an artistic combination of color, size, and texture, as well as continually changing bloom interest. This border is planted with pink and red candytuft, dwarf annual Cape forget-me-not *(Anchusa capensis)*, yellow verbascum, white baby's breath *(Gypsophila)*, yellow yarrow, blue bellflower *(Campanula)*, and yellow evening primrose.

A typical English garden is deceptively informal. In fact, the garden is highly structured by a series of walls, hedges, paths, and borders that form its skeleton. This overview of Vita Sackville-West's Sissinghurst illustrates how the walls and hedges create a series of garden rooms or compartments, each furnished with different plantings to create a distinctive theme. Among the garden themes at Sissinghurst are the famous white garden, an old-fashioned rose garden, a spring garden, a cottage garden, and a garden with a purple border.

▶

Create the look of an English country cottage by growing climbing or rambling roses on the house. This species is "New Dawn," a vigorous, spreading climber. Throughout the summer, it produces double pink blossoms that bleach to white in the sun. The border in the foreground adds to the garden's English ambience.

▼

Use old-fashioned plants, such as these tall, spiky foxgloves combined with Siberian irises, to evoke the essence of an English garden. Other old favorites include sweet peas (particularly fragrant varieties), hollyhocks, bleeding hearts, and columbines.

◀

An arbor arching over the gateway to a cottage garden adds a sense of presence and unity. Soften the structure by growing a vining plant over the trellis, such as this blood-red rose, which contrasts dramatically with the clean white fence and arbor.

"Organized chaos" is one of the best descriptions of an English garden. Here, in a corner of an enclosed secret garden, profusions of flowers trail over and around the lichen-covered stone wall. Notice that the dilapidated gate adds charm to the scene. In a rustic, English-style garden allow some structures to weather, rather than sprucing them up with fresh paint.

The English affection for animals extends to attracting butterflies to their gardens. Here a swallowtail butterfly has alighted on a zinnia. Other flowers that will lure butterflies are asters, borage, lupines, mallows (hollyhocks are included in this family), violets, nasturtiums, marigolds, wisteria, and passionflowers.

Dry stone walls, built of indigenous stone, snake across much of the English countryside. The Cotswolds—a hilly region in the southwest—are especially famous for their stonework. Use stone to create a retaining wall in an English-style garden, and allow plants to tumble over the top. Here yellow alyssum *(Alyssum saxatile)* and *Phlox subulata*, both good rock garden plants, form a colorful cloak covering much of the wall.

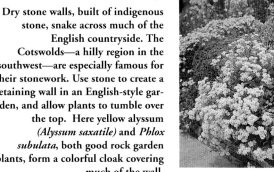

The unpretentious English primrose *(Primula vulgaris)*, which grows wild in that country, has been hybridized with cowslip *(Primula veris)* to produce *Primula polyantha*, and now comes in a wide range of colors. A hardy perennial in all but the coldest parts of North America, the plant is used as an accent in a rock garden or massed as a low border.

▶

The English are famous for their beautiful lawns, which thrive in their temperate climate. To create the look of an English lawn, plant grass as a sea surrounded by a shore of densely planted flowers. The plants around the sides are low in front and taller toward the back. A slightly raised bed just beyond the first low border of flowers contributes to the setting's bowl-like feeling.

▼

The English use rock gardens, or rockeries as they call them, to highlight alpine plant collections. Unfortunately, alpine plants do not grow well in hot, dry American summers, but they do thrive in the Pacific Northwest where the summers are cooler. If you're not in that region, feature dwarf perennial varieties in your rock garden and the smaller minor bulbs.

▼

Design a formal Victorian garden with carpet bedding, massing one type of plant to create a ground-cover effect. To be authentic, the design should include just one or two colors used in a bold but controlled way. Here red *Salvia splendens* is planted in a serpentine shape that undulates toward a Victorian gazebo.

Impressionist painter Claude Monet was influenced by English landscape design. His garden in Giverny, outside Paris, is an amalgam of French formality and English exuberance. Transferring his skill with color on canvas to the garden, Monet matched the flowers to the house with a bed of formal tree roses underplanted with masses of pink geraniums. The low border serves as a substitute for the French boxwood parterre.

▼

Tree-lined roads or paths were common throughout France during Louis XIV's reign and have been maintained throughout the centuries. They were designed to reflect the grandeur of the owner as well as to impose a geometric linearity on the landscape. Border a long drive or walkway with horse chestnuts, birches, lindens, or oaks to create a French-style allée such as this birch one at Hywet Hall, near Akron, Ohio.

▲

Claude Monet gave his version of the French grand allée an English twist by making it less formal. A colorful double herbaceous border forms the sidelines, instead of trees, while arching hoops substitute for a leafy canopy. The edges are softened by nasturtiums, which are allowed to creep right into the path, almost covering it at the height of the season.

◄

Inspired by Italian Renaissance gardens built mainly on hillsides, traditional French-style gardens were adapted to the flat French countryside surrounding Paris and are distinguished by their horizontal lines. They tend to be orderly and formal, with geometric designs emphasizing the triumph of man over nature. Even vegetable gardens, such as this grand one at Château de Villandry, with beds defined by parterres, reflect an intense desire for control. The French use boxwood almost exclusively for their parterres because it is evergreen, long-lived, and slow-growing.

The hilly terrain in Italy lends itself to terraced gardens that start at the top of a hill, where the view is best, and work their way down the slope. Each terrace level is a separate garden room. In the Italian-style garden at Longwood Gardens in Pennsylvania, the stone wall that supports the terrace is decorated with climbing clematis vines interspersed with statuary and fountains. This garden incorporates several traditional Italian elements: stone, restrained use of plants, statuary, and waterworks.

▲
Grottoes, which provide a cool, shady escape from the hot Mediterranean sun, are an important element in grand Italian gardens. Here the idea has been adapted to a California garden. A fountain recess built into the wall creates a cavelike feeling of damp mystery.

▲
A white marble statue set against dark green foliage immediately imbues a garden with an Italian atmosphere. In Italy, statues of people in a garden symbolize man's place in nature. They are placed as focal points, giving a sense of balance and structure to a space, and as a civilized touch at the end of a long, dark green passage.

▲
Italian cypress *(Cupressus sempervirens)*, planted in rows, creates a classic Italian look in mild climate regions such as coastal California, shown here. The hardy columnar-type junipers, such as the different varieties of *Juniperus chinensis* and *Juniperus scopulorum,* are a good substitute where winters are harsh. Flank a path with them, or use a single colonnade to border your property or to define a garden room.

▲

In a traditional Japanese trail garden, a path meanders from one garden space to another, often doubling back on itself in hairpin turns to create the illusion of a larger garden. As it meanders, the path takes on many interesting forms, changing from gravel to cobblestone, or becoming a series of stepping stones, boardwalks, or bridges. Along the edges of the path, pachysandra binds together the elements in the landscape.

▶

A Japanese viewing garden is like a stage set or a picture, with elements carefully placed according to their meaning. Here raked gravel symbolizes an inland sea, while a tableau of boulders and evergreen ground cover *(Ajuga reptans)* suggests a rocky island with curving beaches.

▲

In Japanese gardens, moss along stream banks and lichen on stone are prized as symbols of time and patience. A stone lantern serves as a strong focal point. Candles or light bulbs can illuminate the garden on moonlit nights, at dawn, or at dusk, when subdued lighting heightens the aura of tranquillity.

► If pruned in this way, a Japanese maple *(Acer palmatum)* can provide a visual frame for viewing other sections of the garden. A ground cover of glossy dark green English ivy is an evergreen contrast to the dark branch pattern and golden leaves of the tree, creating a composition that is equally attractive in autumn and winter.

▼ The three important elements in Japanese garden design are green trees and shrubs, water, and stone. Flowers are incidental, so most designs are equally effective in all seasons. In Japan, where there is little space, gardens are condensed, with elements brought close together. This winter tableau of lake, shore, and mountain forming a tiny "cup garden" is small enough to be viewed from the kitchen window.

▲ Japanese gardens are often composed of "cups" on different scales. Cups are formed by hills or mounds that bring focus to a protected central space. A sleek Japanese-style tower can be placed to form the center of a cup. In a cup garden, footpaths around the perimeter of the clearing are used for strolling in contemplation. Here azaleas sheared in mounds and rocks around the pool provide contrasting forms when accentuated by snowfall.

◄ A traditional Japanese garden is designed to encourage *shibusa*, a sense of peace, tranquillity, and refined taste. Many design elements are introduced to slow the pace, encouraging visitors to pause and admire the view. A zigzag bridge is a popular feature, meant to slow down the crossing of boggy ground. The flat span of the bridge serves as an observation platform from which to admire low-lying plants, such as the Japanese iris *(Iris ensata)*. The iris is admired for both its sword-shaped leaves and its spring blue floral display, which is always dramatic but never garish.

Water is an indispensable feature in any Japanese garden. Even in dry gardens, sand or fine gravel is raked in patterns to represent flowing water. Here rocks planted with ferns and azaleas form the shoreline in a dry waterscape. The red lace-leaf Japanese maple (*Acer palmatum* "Dissectum Atropurpureum"), with its fascinating twisted branches, is ideal in a spot like this because it grows slowly and will remain compact.

Even a simple tableau in a Japanese garden is rich with symbolism and design. Here a bamboo pipe drips water into a stone lotus flower basin so slowly that moss can grow despite the overflow. The water trickles over the boulders onto glossy black stones below, which represent a rock fall. Simple shade plantings of hosta and a solitary fern create a tranquil spot where visitors can sit in near-silence listening to the drip of the water.

Create a mound of earth around a Japanese maple and cover it with low-growing ferns and grass that catch the falling autumn leaves. Here a background of bamboo and conifers contrasts with the mound of leaves in color, texture, and line. The color of the leaves is intensified when it rains. Note that the path has been kept raked, adding to the drama of the leaf-covered mound.

An arching moon bridge, here spanning a pebble pool, symbolizes a rainbow in the garden. It is designed purely for aesthetic pleasure and binds elements of the landscape like a giant staple. It is not meant to be walked on.

▲

A Japanese garden design is a highly complex system in which every feature has significance. Even the colors and patterns of the leaves are important. Choose at least one tree, such as this Japanese maple, whose leaves are an art form in themselves.

▲

The Japanese use ornamental grasses, such as this *Miscanthus sinensis* "Gracillimus," sparingly, but to great effect. Here a solitary clump is like a living waterfall arching into the quiet pool. Falling in a fountainlike form, the grass makes a gentle rustling sound, similar to water, when stirred by the breeze. The golden color of the grass and the red of the maple contrast beautifully with the predominantly evergreen surroundings.

◄

Break the monotony of a horizontal design in a Japanese garden with taller shrubs. Here the glossy leaves of a rhododendron and the delicate foliage of a lace-leaf Japanese maple (*Acer palmatum* "Dissectum Viridie") arch protectively toward the stone basin, forming a frame to the scene and adding height to the pachysandra ground cover.

Unlike predominantly green Italian gardens, Spanish gardens vibrate with color, both from bold flowering plants, such as this bougainvillea vine, and from brightly colored architectural features, such as colored stucco, decorative wall tiles, and red-tiled roofs and wall caps. Plant bright tropical and subtropical flowers to create an exuberant Mediterranean feeling in a garden, even if your house is not Spanish in style.

▼

Place a fountain as a central feature in an enclosed courtyard to create a Spanish garden feeling. Here, in the Carmel Mission, the tile-capped wall forming the pool doubles as a seat. Spanish-style gardens are particularly popular in Florida, California, and the Southwest, where the climate approximates that of Spain and where Spanish influence is part of the region's history.

◀

Celebrate the sound and cooling effect of water in a hot-climate Spanish-style garden with a combination of pools, ponds, fountains, and waterways. The famous Moorish gardens at the Alhambra fortress in Granada, Spain, inspired this long, narrow waterway at Longue Vue Gardens in Louisiana.

▲

A garden seat decorated with painted tiles is a wonderful accent in a Spanish-style garden. Tiles such as these are available in Mexico and are imported from Spain and Portugal. Also use tile to adorn walls, fountains, and stairs (see page 132).

Regional Gardens

ARDEN STYLES DIFFER from one North American region to another, just as climate and topography do. As a rule, gardens tend to reflect the cultural characteristics of the region's first settlers, as well as a range of historical, social, and lifestyle variables. A traditional southern garden is as different from a typical California garden as a Japanese garden is from a French one.

Plant Hardiness

It is important to understand your region's climate and soil conditions because both affect plant hardiness. Very different climates exist from region to region. Along the coast of the Pacific Northwest, winters are damp and the climate is similar to that of England, whereas the Gulf states, the Southwest, and southern California have very warm summers and mild winters, and southern Florida is tropical. More than three-quarters of North America experiences snow with prolonged freezing temperatures in winter.

Plant hardiness is determined primarily by the degree of cold and freezing temperatures the plant can tolerate, but also by its exposure to winds and snow cover. In North America's northern states and high-elevation areas, plants generally die from dehydration, caused by cold winds. To prevent dehydration, put susceptible plants in sheltered locations, spray the trunks and branches with an anti-desiccant in early winter, wrap them, and water them adequately if natural rainfall is light before winter dormancy. A lack of an insulating snow cover in cold regions can also cause dehydration, but a substitute can be provided with organic mulch. Cover the soil with straw, pine needles, or

shredded leaves. Mulch is best applied after the ground freezes, since the object is to keep the ground and plants dormant until the spring thaw. The alternate thawing and freezing of the ground tend to put an enormous stress on plants, creating heavy losses.

The U.S. Department of Agriculture has divided North America into hardiness zones, numbered from 1 (including parts of Alaska, where frost can occur every month of the year) to 10 (the Florida Keys and San Diego, where frost is rare). But even frost-free areas have distinct differences, largely due to humidity and to rainfall patterns. For example, coconut palms thrive in southern Florida, but perish in southern California for lack of humidity and summer rainfall, although both regions fall into the same hardiness zone.

With the exception of California, it is fairly easy to determine which hardiness zone you live in by looking at the USDA's zone map—especially the newly revised version, which is more detailed. California has so many microclimates it's better to refer to a copy of the Western Garden Book (Lane Publishing Co.), in which you will find more detailed zone maps of the state. No matter where you live, however, use the zone maps only as a guide. Nothing beats asking a local nursery, farmers, and gardening neighbors about what can and can't be grown and other vital information, such as first and last frost dates and the most troublesome pests and diseases.

Soil Types

Soil types are generally classified by their consistency—sandy, clay, or loam. Sandy soil is made up of coarse soil particles that have poor moisture-holding ability, while clay particles are tiny

Regional Gardens 33

and clump together into a heavy, cold mass that plant roots have difficulty penetrating. The happy medium—loam—is achieved by having a good concentration of humus. The remedy for improving both sand and clay soil is the same—add heavy doses of organic matter, such as compost, peat, leaf mold, or well-decomposed animal manure.

Soil can also be acid or alkaline. Certain plants (such as hollies and rhododendrons) favor a highly acid soil, while other plants (such as bluebonnets and Indian paintbrush) prefer it alkaline. Soils in areas with regular rainfall patterns and forested areas tend to be acid (almost all of Pennsylvania, for example, has acid soil), while desert areas and prairies tend to be alkaline. Most plants prefer a soil close to neutral or only slightly acid. The remedy for highly acid soils is an application of lime, while alkaline soil can be corrected with sulphur. A soil test is the most accurate way to tell how much of either is needed.

California

Blessed with a temperate Mediterranean climate throughout its most populated coastal areas, California has evolved a unique garden style that reflects a preference for an outdoor lifestyle, a need to accommodate the ubiquitous automobile, and a limited amount of garden space.

One of the most influential landscape architects in California history was Thomas Church. Working from the 1930s until his death in 1978, Church defined what is now considered the archetypal California garden look. Focusing on the San Francisco Bay Area, he paved surfaces and planted ground covers to reduce maintenance, used screens and changes in level to create a sense of private garden rooms, and, on very small lots, employed illusions to give the appearance of more space. His garden designs—which always included a patio for sitting—functioned as outdoor rooms, extending the living space.

Ideally, Church preferred projects where he was called in at the same time as the architect. Together, they could position the house with views and garden in mind. Then, working closely with the client, Church designed a garden that was integrated with the house and its surroundings.

Church's philosophy of garden design is best described by the title of his landmark book, *Gardens Are for People.* He designed beautiful spaces, but never at the expense of function. His gardens were ergonomic, conceived for people to enjoy within the context of the greater California landscape. As he put it, landscaping is "logical, down-to-earth, and aimed at making your plot of ground produce exactly what you want and need from it."

Church's followers continue in this tradition. As spare land grows scarcer and more expensive and as lot sizes shrink, landscape architects are responding with more complex designs, such as a swimming pool constructed over the edge of a cliff. As you may imagine, such designs often require sophisticated technology and materials to implement, but the goal is always simple: to extend the usable living space of the house into the outdoors.

Like space, water is a precious commodity in California, and in increasingly short supply. To make up for a lack of rain and natural streams and ponds, water is often celebrated in gardens. Like the ancient Persians and the Moors in Spain, designers introduce water as a soothing, cooling element and use it in various forms, from ornamental waterways and fountains (where water is circulated with pumps) to swimming pools and spas. By the same token, responsible landscape architects use drought-tolerant and native plants, and nurseries have responded by propagating them en masse. This includes some unusual drought-tolerant plants that were once difficult to find, such as obscure species of agaves, aloes, euphorbias, sedums, and ornamental grasses.

The California climate is one of the few in the country that allows for year-round gardening. In the southern coastal area, tropical flowers bloom in midwinter, while inland oranges ripen within sight of snow-capped peaks. It is a region offering rich and diverse horticultural possibilities.

Southwest

The Southwest—encompassing Arizona, New Mexico, and parts of Texas—is a wide open region with sweeping desert landscapes, accented by ancient mountain ranges rising up out of the flatlands. The air is hot and dry, and in places the ground consists of caliche, an impenetrable substance. The nineteenth-century statesman Daniel Webster disparaged the area, referring to it as "a barren waste of prairie dogs, cactus, and shifting sands," but opinions and experiences differ. New Mexico is nicknamed the "Land of Enchantment," and Arizona is a major agricultural state.

Inhabited first by Indians and then settled by the Spaniards, who established Sante Fe years before the Pilgrims landed at Plymouth Rock, the Southwest has a garden style that reflects these two cultures, as well as the rigors of a hot, dry climate and stony, alkaline soil.

Houses built of adobe—a sun-dried clay that stays cool on hot days, but also retains warmth on cold winter nights—have their roots in ancient Pueblo Indian architecture and are still popular today. The Spanish settlers imitated the Pueblo style, adding their own innovations such as patios and wrought-iron balconies, structures that form the basis of many southwestern gardens. Patios, which are a haven from the hot sun and drying winds, are often surrounded by adobe walls and paved with terra-cotta tiles. Red clay pots filled with palms, cacti, or blooming, heat-loving annuals are used as accents.

A hot region that gets little rain (Arizona boasts 292 days of sunshine a year), the Southwest is ideal for growing cacti and other drought-tolerant plants. Water-hungry lawns are rare. Instead, people create ground covers of decorative stone or gravel and use large boulders or a random plant for an accent.

that the two major styles influencing Pacific Northwest gardens are Japanese and English.

Although typical gardens are not necessarily laid out and planted in the Japanese style, many have an Oriental element, such as full-size trees pruned in the bonsai style or in a Japanese topiary form. Azaleas and rhododendrons, both favored in Japanese gardens, flourish here.

The English influence can be found both in the plants and in the garden styles. The climate makes it possible to grow certain plant types, such as alpines, that won't perform well in other parts of the country. Primroses, delphiniums, mecanopsis poppies, and Exbury azaleas are a few examples of flowers that thrive in the cool, moist summers and relatively temperate winters of the Pacific Northwest. Laburnum, a tree that graces English gardens with long golden panicles of flowers in May, is spectacular in this region, grown as a small tree or trained across walls and over hoops to create an arbor. Wildflowers enjoy a prolonged blooming season and are ideal mixed with old-fashioned perennials to create a charming cottage garden. As in England, lawns are easy to grow in the Northwest. You will commonly see dinner plate–size dahlias in many colors and forms, planted as a cheerful rim to a free-form lawn.

Washington is known as the "Evergreen State," because of its vast forests of firs, hemlocks, and other cone-bearing trees. Both here and in neighboring Oregon, the planting of woodland gardens—with ferns, rhododendrons, and azaleas—is a natural landscape trend. In addition, many gardeners plant native wildflowers, such as lupine and avalanche lilies *(Erythronium),* which are unique to the region.

Midwest

Early settlers in the Midwest planted traditional European gardens—in a formalized style with parterres. But early in this century Jens Jensen, a Dane who settled in Chicago, began a landscape reformation, introducing a new garden vision for this region. For Jensen, the European garden styles exemplified the autocratic rule of rich over poor, while the wide open prairies of the Midwest represented the freedom and opportunity in the United States. His landscapes were designed to celebrate these prairie qualities.

For wealthy midwestern clients—such as the Fords and Armours—Jensen designed unpretentious gardens, using native plants in a landscaped environment that echoed their natural setting. Instead of a vista across a lawn, he created an open meadow filled with prairie wildflowers; instead of importing temperamental woody plant specimens, he planted a grove of native trees—such as osage orange—to create a parklike setting. His gardens were for strolling, with rustic wooden bridges and stone paths leading through woodland. To add mystery and an illusion of greater size to a garden, he designed lawns that curved out of sight, drawing the observer into the landscape.

Light and shadow, as they change throughout the day, were

These neutral backgrounds are ideal to set off the fascinating shapes and colors of agaves, euphorbias, yuccas, and cacti, which grow easily in this environment. If grass is planted, it's usually a small patch of a heat-tolerant type such as Bermuda, St. Augustine, or zoysia.

Gardening is a favorite winter pastime in the Southwest. When the air cools and the annual 10 to 15 inches of rain fall, people tend their vegetable gardens and prepare flower beds for a burst of bloom in the early spring. By late spring the rains stop and the sun persists, withering the blossoms and leaving only heat-hardy, water-resistant plants.

In places where the rock-hard caliche makes it impossible to dig the earth, southwesterners adapt by building raised beds. The depth of the top soil depends on what is being planted, but 8 inches is a minimum. These raised beds, often contained by low walls, assume many forms, from a simple bed outlined with local stone to brick or adobe planters built to match the house.

Water is a scarce resource and a treasured element in the Southwest, as it is in California. Swimming pools are common, as are fountains and decorative ponds. Some pools are designed to blend with the wild landscape beyond, as shown on page 20; others are often distinctly Spanish, decorated with brightly painted tiles.

Pacific Northwest

Fine natural harbors make Washington State a major gateway to the Orient, and the ties of commerce extend to landscape design. The northern climate west of the Cascade mountain range is similar to that of England. It is understandable, then, important features in Jensen's gardens. Many vistas were oriented to show off the rising or setting sun. His overall goal was to put the city dweller back in touch with nature's rhythms and patterns.

Not many of Jensen's gardens remain, but his spirit is alive in his successors, be they professional designers or home gardeners, who plant prairie gardens filled with native grasses and flowers in an informal setting. These natural-looking gardens are much easier to maintain than traditional gardens are, less expensive to plant, and look good throughout the year because the plants are adapted to the climate and seasons.

Northeast

The first settlers in the Northeast found a densely forested land that seemed to sprout stones each time the land was tilled in the spring. They cleared the forests to grow crops, and they harvested the stones for building walls and shelters or used them for rock gardens. These stone walls and rock gardens, originally a method of using the unwanted crop of stones, are now a much-loved hallmark of old northeastern gardens.

While seasons blur in many parts of the country, in the Northeast they are distinct, which means they must be considered when designing the landscape and selecting plants. The growing season is relatively short, with early bulbs such as snowdrops and aconites making an appearance around mid-March, after possibly 6 months of freezing temperatures. Plants must be hardy to withstand such protracted periods of cold. Garden features such as evergreen hedges, walls, benches, ponds, trees with striking forms, and statuary are the source of interest during the winter months, when flowers and foliage are gone.

Come spring and summer, traditional country gardens are abloom with beds of annuals, perennials, and herbs—often mixed together in sweet abandon; vines encircle front doors, and rolling lawns lead to deciduous woodland beyond.

Northeastern gardens have their roots in the styles of Europe and Colonial America. Today, innovators plan gardens that use the site as is, rather than clearing and grading it to achieve a bare site for a traditional garden. Instead of removing all trees, today's gardeners are apt to use them as part of the landscape, seeding wildflowers and using shade-loving plants to create naturalistic woodland gardens.

Weekend vacation homes, located in the mountains, at the seaside, and in rural communities abound in this region. The gardens in these places reflect people's need for a small plot of land to cultivate with a minimum amount of effort.

South

Landscape design in the South ranges from the expansive scale of plantations to the tiny, formal city gardens of Charleston, South Carolina, and the flower-laden balconies of New Orleans. The climate varies from subtropical in the northern parts of the

region to tropical in southern Florida. This is an area renowned for its brilliant flowers, including Indian azaleas, camellias, wisteria, jasmine, and crape myrtle.

Much of garden design in the South is geared toward making summer heat tolerable. Plantations feature lawns that sweep down to a lake or river, arched over with groves of trees. The oak is valued not only for its deep root system, but also for its spreading foliage canopy. Wrought iron adorns porches and balconies, creating a decorative shelter that allows breezes to flow, and the bricks in the walls are often staggered in an ornamental pattern, with holes to increase the air circulation. Water, in the form of a large lake on a plantation or a fountain or pool in a patio garden, is prized for its cooling effects.

Southern gardens tend to be traditional and formal. The plantation gardens, many of which are now open to the public, were developed in the mid-eighteenth century when the owners admired French formal garden designs. Geometric flower beds often radiate out from a central axis, and as a focal point, zoysia lawns are often outlined in patterned brick walks. The city gardens are small and walled, with holly clipped into topiary forms and fragrant vines such as jasmine scrambling up and over the walls. Boxwood parterres outline beds, and cherubs or nymphs are used as decorative sculptural accents.

The tropical region of Florida has its own garden style, echoing the Mediterranean designs of Spain and Italy. Tropical plants abound and are incorporated into Spanish-style courtyards and terraces that recall their original Spanish settlers. Bold-colored flowers such as bougainvillea vines, ginger, and bromeliads (especially tillandsias) stand out against dark green foliage and pastel-colored walls.

If you are moving from one region to another, look in the local library for a good regional garden book to learn what garden designs work and which plants survive (the *Western Garden Book,* for example, has sold more copies than any other garden book in North America). It is also a good idea to visit the office of your county agent for free or inexpensive booklets about local garden problems. And if there is a state horticultural society or botanical garden, find out if regular garden tours are offered that will allow you to view both new and historical garden designs.

Soften an expanse of hardscape by interplanting paving stones with a ground cover, such as mat-forming Roman chamomile. The leaves release an applelike scent when crushed (in Greek "chamomile" means "ground apple") and as Shakespeare's Falstaff remarked, "The more it is trodden on the faster it grows."

Thomas Church was a leading California landscape architect from the 1930s until his death in 1978. He made an important mark on California garden design by using level changes and trompe l'oeil trelliswork to make small spaces feel bigger. With paving, he created low-maintenance garden rooms and, whenever possible, designed them to accommodate existing trees, giving the setting a sense of age and permanence.

Spanish architecture and garden design came to California in the late eighteenth century, and the style has endured. Enhance a shady, enclosed Spanish-style courtyard with plants that need little light, such as these blooming clivias. The old, twisted branches of a wisteria vine soften architectural lines when in leaf and bloom and provide a sculptural interest in winter.

◄

In California, where water is scarce, create a drought-tolerant version of a cottage garden with dry-climate flowering perennials and shrubs, such as sage, French lavender, white Matilija poppy, santolina, white flowering penstemon, oleander, yellow yarrow, and statice. Here junipers, citrus trees, and an olive tree add structure to the design, as does the dry "watercourse" of boulders flowing down the hill into the curving stone path.

▼

Hillside gardens are another challenge in California. Use a checkerboard design of silver- and green-leafed santolina for erosion control. Both evergreen and summer-flowering shrubs are especially good for coastal areas because they can tolerate salt, wind, and drought. These yellow flowers are combined with purple flowers of French lavender, statice, and ice plants to create a dynamic color combination.

Even when water is in short supply, you can have a flower garden if you plan carefully. Here in the Blake House garden in Berkeley, California, a small lily pool is beautifully landscaped with a variety of drought-tolerant annuals and perennials, many with silver foliage. Creeping thyme, lavender, and blue fescue edge the pool. The deep green yew hedge makes an ideal backdrop for the silver artemesia and santolina interplanted with annuals such as orange-flowering celosia and blue ageratum. Lemon trees, which have been pruned to leave space underneath, add height to the scene as well as bright yellow fruit in season.

▶

▲

Retain the soil on a steep, sunny bank with a vivid orange-red carpet of dewflower *(Drosanthemum speciosum).* Like most ice plants, it blooms in the sun and requires little water once established. In this garden the red flowers against the silvery blue agave provide a striking color combination.

▶

Botanists have found Australia and South Africa to be rich sources for plant materials that do well in California. Here orange ice plants, red gazanias, and yellow African daisies live together as happily in the dry California climate as they do in their native South Africa.

▼

Where the climate is right, plant a lush tropical garden with a collection of palm trees. A diverse family, palms come in varieties ranging from very short to many stories tall. Some are sensitive to cold, others grow outdoors as far north as southern Oregon on the West Coast and Williamsburg, Virginia, on the East Coast. Even a small space can house many palm trees. Here they form a beautifully textured private screen.

▼

Create a dazzling, low-maintenance meadow garden with drought-tolerant flowers such as these gazanias and *Ursinia calenduliflora.* Gazanias and ursinias, which both bloom in late spring through early summer, are perennial plants in warm climates; grow them as annuals if frosts are severe.

▲

Citrus trees in full fruit, sometimes seen with snow-topped mountains in the background, are a hallmark of California gardens. If space is a problem, plant a dwarf variety such as this Chinotto orange. A particularly handsome plant, it grows in a rounded symmetrical shape and produces lots of sweet-scented flowers in spring and clusters of oranges in winter. The juicy but sour fruit, which is prized in Italy for making candy, remains on the tree almost year-round, adding to its ornamental value. Here *Rosa banksiae*, particularly well-suited to the California climate, makes a stunning floral backdrop to the Chinotto oranges.

◄

Despite the trend toward smaller lots in California, there is almost always room for a swimming pool and bubbling spa. Tuck a small pool right up against the edge of the property, with a dense screen of evergreen foliage secluding the space from the outside world. A natural stone edge on the far side of the pool acts as a retaining wall, making the pool feel even more protected and removed.

►

If blessed with a cliff-front view, allow your garden to follow the contours of the land. This lawn, with a low balustrade for safety, is planted right up to the edge of the cliff so that the green grass above and blue sea below appear to merge. The upper-level deck also stretches out toward the view and provides an almost aerial vantage point, mimicking the curve of the cliff edge below.

◄

In a seaside garden, where wind and salt spray can defeat tender plants, create a tapestry of drought-tolerant ornamental grasses. Here soft pink panicles of sesleria make a pretty foil to the red spikes of New Zealand flax *(Phormium)* in front. Behind the miscanthus, rainbow-colored varieties of *Phormium* edge a wide swath of blue fescue.

Turquoise is the traditional color for a pool, but tiles in a deep shade, such as this royal blue, blend best with the southwestern landscape and reduce glare from strong sun. The pool also matches the sky, while the boulders set in the patio echo the mountains beyond. Palo verde trees *(Cercidium)*, growing along the wall and to the right, are native to southwestern deserts.

Turn a desert environment into a sea of blooms with a meadow of drought-tolerant wildflowers, such as this mix of African daisies and blue flax growing in an apricot orchard.

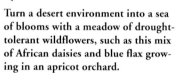

Much of the soil in the Southwest is composed of caliche, a stone-hard material that requires a pickax to break it up. Instead of fighting this hardpan, build raised beds filled with top soil. These herb beds, which have been outlined with local stone, are raised about 1 foot above the impenetrable ground.

Adobe, terra-cotta, and red brick are commonly used in southwestern home architecture and gardens, reflecting a Spanish influence. A brick wall, punctuated with decorative holes made from roofing tiles, joins the house, both physically and by common materials, to the enclosed patio. Pots filled to capacity with blooming annuals add color in a paved area.

To create an easy-maintenance garden, naturalize it with a profusion of plants that do well in the Southwest and that don't need pruning or shaping. In this informal garden the shaggy white heads of a potted old-man cactus *(Cephalocereus senilis)* stand in contrast to the yellow cassia shrubs against the wall, prickly pear cactus *(Opuntia robusta)*, and clumps of yellow-flowering euphorbia.

Celebrate the desert spring with an early planting of pansies and Iceland poppies *(Papaver nudicaule)*, which bloom in March before the summer heat. A perennial rye lawn, seeded in the fall, also remains green during the cool months. Once the nights get hot, the lawn will die back, to be supplanted by the dormant warm-season grasses: Bermuda, St. Augustine, and zoysia.

Native to Asia Minor, ranunculus is a striking spring-blooming flower that flourishes in the southwestern climate. Choose the largest, plumpest corms, and in October or November plant them with a little bonemeal, about 1 to 2 inches deep and about 6 inches apart. The toes should point down. Unless the winter is very dry, they do not need watering. The corms will rot if they get too wet.

Because water is precious in the Southwest, use it for very special effects. A small pool, pond, or fountain, surrounded by cacti, succulents, and agave with many different leaf forms and colors, creates a drought-tolerant garden oasis.

▲

Laburnum, or golden-chain tree, is a dazzling plant in bloom and does particularly well in the cool, moist climate of the Pacific Northwest. Grow these trees in parallel rows to create an avenue lined with sunny flowers. Laburnum trees are also good for espaliers. Shown here is *Laburnum* × *watereri*, a hybrid between two hardy laburnum species whose flower clusters grow up to 20 inches long.

►

These pine trees have been pruned so the branches resemble layers of clouds floating in the sky, reflecting the strong Oriental influence in Pacific Northwest gardening. The two pruned pines stand next to a conical cedar and blue spruce, providing an interesting contrast in form and color. Junipers covering the ground continue the soothing conifer motif.

▲

In the Pacific Northwest, wildflowers that have a short bloom season in hot climates begin flowering in May and continue through summer. Usually grown as annuals, Iceland poppies overwinter in this region, maintaining a rosette of leaves throughout the cold months. Other wildflowers that flourish in the Pacific Northwest are California poppies, wild lupines, and foxgloves.

▶

The climate along the coast of Oregon is surprisingly mild, similar to that of England and Japan. In protected areas, semitropical microclimates make it possible to grow a variety of unexpected plants, including these blue dracaena palm trees *(Cordyline indivisa)*, which also do well in salty shoreline conditions. In this garden at Shore Acres, Oregon, a Japanese cup design has been created with a pond as the bottom of the cup and the path around the pond as the lip. A pair of herons has been placed in the center as a focal point.

▼

Local crafts, so readily available in the Pacific Northwest, are wonderful decorations for the garden. In this Japanese garden, two salmon pop their heads out of a river of stones, creating a charming, whimsical tableau. A Japanese maple *(Acer palmatum)* arches protectively over the scene.

▲

The Pacific Northwest climate is particularly conducive to growing a wide range of plants. Cool-climate, moisture-loving plants that thrive in this region would never do well in hotter, dryer parts of North America. A "Sappho" rhododendron, for example, not normally suited to this continent, flourishes in this Portland, Oregon, garden. Lawns are also easier to grow in the Pacific Northwest than elsewhere in the United States.

▶

Ferns and rhododendrons grow better in parts of the Pacific Northwest than they do anywhere else in North America. Use the hospitable environment to cultivate a woodland garden featuring a wide variety of rhododendrons, azaleas, and ferns.

◄ Ornamental grasses tolerant of drought, wind, and cold are a good choice for Midwest gardens because they will survive the sweeping winds and hot summers typical of the region. Here large clumps of *Miscanthus sinensis* "Arabesque" and "Cabaret" flank two lounge chairs, creating a feathery protective screen in this secluded patio.

► Perennial prairie flowers, such as the native yellow sunflowers and purple coneflowers *(Echinacea purpurea)* growing in this informal border, are charming and in harmony with the Midwest region. Introduce annuals, such as the red zinnias in front of the sunflowers and orange French marigolds beside the coneflowers, for a contrast in texture and color.

► Celebrate the farming heritage of the Midwest by using an attractive farm implement, such as an antique plow, as a garden ornament. The snap-dragon-like flower shown here is Linaria "Fairy Bouquet," an early-flowering, easy-to-grow annual propagated from seed.

▲ If the wind is strong in your area, plant trees as a windbreak to create a sheltered garden where sensitive flowers can grow. Here baby's breath *(Gypsophilia)*, purple loosestrife *(Lythrum)*, and rudbeckias grow happily under the protection of tall American arborvitae trees—native evergreen conifers that cushion the force of high winds.

In a region with pronounced seasonal changes, a strong structural design helps a garden be attractive any time of year. Here at Deerfield garden in Pennsylvania, the gentle curve of a pond is echoed in the line formed by nearby shrubs. The lawn serves as a path, continuing beyond the water and drawing the viewer's eye to the distant vista. The bridge also attracts attention and becomes a good transitional device, connecting the wild woods beyond the spillway to the more cultivated sweep of lawn. The result is a pleasing tension between cultivated spaces to the left and unbridled nature to the right.

In spring, blooming pink and red azaleas contrast with the fresh green foliage. The pond picks up reflections, emphasizing the straight trunks of the dominant trees. In summer, when the flowers have faded, the spot is a lush bower.

The emphasis at Deerfield changes in autumn. Instead of bright flowers, it is the treetops, aflame with seasonal oranges, reds, and golds, that make it so breathtaking. Although the lawn is usually kept raked, leaves are left to carpet the water with a floating design.

In winter, when foliage and color are gone, Deerfield garden's structural design is enhanced all the more by snow. Dark trees are etched starkly against a steely sky, while the pond is transformed into a metallic mirror. Even in a small garden, trees and shrubs with fascinating skeletal structures placed beside a pond are an interesting focal point in winter.

▲
When building structures in a garden, use materials that blend with the surroundings or are in keeping with a local style. In this Pennsylvania garden, a pond was built of local stone, in keeping with the Quaker tradition. The pond fits into its setting and combines well with the other stone structures on the property.

▶
If you are fortunate enough to have a collapsed dry stone wall on an unused portion of your property, move the stones and rebuild the wall as a feature in your garden. This dry stone wall topped with blooming sedum is a charming rustic divider between two sections of garden.

▲
Evoke a sense of country with a comfortable Adirondack chair placed to enjoy a vista. Originally designed by furniture makers in the Adirondack mountains, these chairs have a deep, comfortable seat and clean lines that make them popular throughout North America.

Plant perennial chrysanthemums for a dependable display of color in autumn. At the end of the flowering season, cut the plants back to the ground. Then, the following summer, when they start growing again, pinch off the bud tips to encourage branching and more blooms. Many mums grow tall, so they may require staking to keep them from drooping on the ground.

Transform a neglected roadside spot into a pretty focal point with a mass planting of creeping phlox *(Phlox stolonifera)*. This evergreen spreading perennial, which is hardy from zones 4 to 8, produces a carpet of small pale blue flowers in early summer. A variety known as "Blue Ridge" blooms in lavender blue; another called "Bruce's White" has white flowers. All types do best in sun or semishade, in moist, well-draining soil.

For summer flowers in a partially shady spot, plant hydrangea. Depending on the variety, the large bloom clusters come in white, pink, or blue. If grown in acid soil, hydrangea flowers tend to be blue, in alkaline soil they tend to be pink. It is even possible for a hydrangea plant to have pink flowers one year and blue the next.

Lilacs, which thrive on deep winter chill, are ideal to grow in the Northeast. Each species has distinct qualities—varying sizes, forms, growth habits, and bloom times—that may be an asset to your landscape. The Chinese lilac *(Syringa chinensis)* shown here, blooms in May, and is considered more graceful than the common lilac *(Syringa vulgaris)*.

Plan a garden for a weekend vacation home that can be maintained in two days a week or less. The combination of dahlias, phlox, marigolds, and petunias shown here has an informal, welcoming feeling and makes a showy, colorful display. The small, contained bed requires little work—an ideal situation for a second home.

Allow coastline gardens to merge with the wild environment. This seaside garden nudges right up against the boulders of a rugged Rhode Island shore. Masses of rock create a clear delineation between private and public land, but the patches of lawn that have seeded themselves on the boulders blur that distinction. The resulting contrasts are emotionally and visually exciting.

The Northeast is one of the most heavily wooded regions in the country. Instead of cutting down your trees to create a traditional garden, consider your wooded lot a valuable asset and work within the constraints of shade. With minimal tree thinning or branch pruning, a wooded area can be transformed into a natural-looking, colorful garden. Here a lawn serves as a path into the woods, while blooming forget-me-nots and azaleas add spring beauty to the scene.

▲

When the climate is hot, nothing is as soothing as a reflecting pool or pond in a garden. The scale here is grand, with the house sited midway up the hill so that the view is framed by the trees. If the house were sited nearer the top, the view would be of treetops instead. The palmettos growing on tiny islands in this pond are indigenous to Florida, as is the Spanish moss dripping from the trees.

▶

Instead of hauling away an old split log, use it as a planter. In this boggy garden, creeping phlox is tucked into the opening in the log to create a deliberately naturalistic planting. The baby palmettos growing among the azaleas will eventually grow to more than 20 feet tall, adding to the view from the gazebo.

▲

Native to Mexico, poinsettias *(Euphorbia pulcherrima)* will thrive outdoors in frost-free areas. After your potted plants have stopped blooming, cut the stalks back to 4 or 6 inches and plant them in a well-drained, sunny location. Once they are established, prune the plants every 2 months to promote a bushy form. You can also train them as small trees by allowing just one stalk to grow tall before it branches out at the top.

A formal garden outlined in boxwood parterres evokes the Old World influence common in southern gardens. Include an ornamental tree, such as this fringe tree *(Chionanthus virginicus)*, to add height to the design. The various azaleas here were chosen because their flowering time coincides with that of the tree.

A heat-lover, crape myrtle *(Lagerstroemia indica)* is ideal for a summer bloom in the South. Its long flowering period runs from July to September, when the plant is covered in clusters of small, crinkled crepelike flowers. Colors range from white to pink, red, lavender, and even variegated pink and white, and varieties range from dwarf shrubs to small trees. To prevent mildew, spray just before the plants flower.

A Biblical theme garden features plants mentioned in the Bible. In this example at Magnolia Gardens in Charleston, South Carolina, the theme is further strengthened by the form. A low parterre grows in the shape of a Star of David with a replica of Michelangelo's statue of David in the center, while the path forms a cross. A statue of the Madonna graces a cross-shaped planter in the middle. Plants you might consider for a Biblical garden are figs, dates, palms, olives, lilies, and various healing herbs.

Whenever possible, preserve a grand old tree. Here in New Orleans, the street curb and sidewalk take a jog to accommodate this stately tree, which is rightly viewed as a treasure. You can encourage moss to grow in shady spots by creating a damp, acidic environment. Exposed tree roots like these also make excellent planters for minor bulbs, such as squill. Simply place the bulbs among the roots and fill in the gaps with soil (page 166).

Allow cooling breezes to flow into your garden by building a brick wall with spaces in it. The effect is pretty and lacy, as well as practical. Walls such as these are a trademark of southern gardens, where good air circulation is essential during muggy summer months.

There are scores of magnolia species, but the one that most typifies the South is *Magnolia grandiflora*, a large evergreen tree with wide glossy leaves and enormous, fragrant, creamy white blossoms. The trees are reliably hardy as far north as Philadelphia (zone 7) if they are in a sheltered spot, such as next to a warm wall. Prolonged extreme cold will kill mature plants.

The southern live oak *(Quercus virginiana)*, native to the eastern United States, is one of the best landscape trees for southern gardens. The oaks, which ultimately grow to 60 feet with a spreading, heavy-limbed crown, are an excellent source of shade. These trees are evergreen in warm regions and thrive in deep, rich soil with plenty of water. When grown in this combination of conditions they put down deep root systems, which make them extremely solid. Hurricane Hugo toppled many pine trees in Charleston's Magnolia Gardens, but the live oaks remained standing.

Use wrought-iron railings and trellis-work to frame a beautiful view. The lacy patterns are remarkably decorative but are also practical in the South, because they allow cooling breezes to flow through.

▲

For a short but glorious burst of color in May, plant Dutch amaryllis *(Hip-peastrum)* in your landscape. These bulbs have to be grown indoors in pots in most of the country, but in the South they will overwinter outdoors in sandy soil. After the bloom, which lasts about 10 days, the foliage will die back until the following spring. Snails adore both the tops and bulbs of these plants, so protect them carefully. Successful hybridizing of the amaryllis has produced a range of colors such as dark red, scarlet, orange, salmon, white, and pink, with many variations and combinations.

◄

Caladiums (rainbow plants), which come in brilliant color combinations, rival most flowering plants. Use them in beds, borders, or pots. A heat-tolerant plant that likes bright, indirect light, caladium provides a splendid leaf display until the plant dies back for a 4-month period of winter dormancy. When the leaves turn brown, pull the plants and store the bulbs in burlap bags until the following spring. To keep caladiums healthy, fertilize three times a year, in spring, midsummer, and early autumn.

Plant Theme Gardens

$\mathcal{J}$UST AS SOME people collect stamps or coins, others collect plants. The wide range of species, varieties, shapes, and sizes in many plant families captures the imagination of enthusiasts who want to have them all.

One of the first plant collectors was the French empress Josephine Bonaparte, wife of Napoleon. At Malmaison, her mansion near Paris, she cultivated an extensive rose garden, which included every rose known at the time. She used her position shamelessly, going as far as to confiscate any horticultural bounty found on captured English ships while her husband was at war with England. She even managed to import roses directly from Britain during that time, in spite of the war. Josephine documented her cherished plants by employing the well-known botanical artist Pierre-Joseph Redoute to make accurate pictures of each rose. Their work helped to establish the French as leaders in the field of rose breeding and hybridizing.

Varieties of Plant Theme Gardens

Out of collections like Josephine's roses emerge plant theme gardens. Some of the most famous gardens in the world base their reputation on one plant family. Magnolia Gardens near Charleston, South Carolina, and Callaway Gardens in Pine Mountain, Georgia, are both renowned for their azalea displays in early spring, while in Montclair, New Jersey, the Presby Iris Memorial Garden attracts thousands of admirers for the 3- to 4-week period around Memorial Day when hundreds of varieties of iris are in bloom. On the opposite coast, Descanso Gardens in La Canada, California, is a mecca for those who want to see camellias.

Some large estate gardens have several plant theme garden rooms. In addition to their famous topiary, Ladew Topiary Gardens near Baltimore, Maryland, include twenty-two such garden rooms, including peony, iris, herb, rose, wildflower, and water lily gardens. At Huntington Botanical Gardens in San Marino, California, visitors can stroll through 130 acres of theme gardens devoted to roses, camellias, and herbs, as well as a Shakespearean garden filled with plants mentioned in his plays and poems. Most impressive of all, perhaps, is a 12-acre hillside planted entirely with thousands of cacti and desert succulents.

On a smaller scale, suburban gardeners who have a passion for the one-plant family, but don't want to devote their entire garden to it, can confine the plants to one section, creating a small plant theme garden. In this way they can have the pleasure of collecting, while maintaining an aesthetically varied landscape.

In general, plant theme gardens look better when the main plant family is combined with other plants that are complementary in some way. The desert garden at Huntington Botanical Gardens uses the cactus as its main theme, but is also planted with agaves, yuccas, bromeliads, euphorbias, and drought-tolerant flowering trees such as the floss silk tree *(Chorisia speciosa)* and ponytail palm *(Beaucarnea recurvata)*.

The prettiest rose gardens usually have a background of dark green foliage—such as a yew hedge or holly topiary—to display the plants to best advantage. Old-fashioned roses, many of which bloom just once in spring, work well surrounded with summer-blooming annuals and perennials to give interest to the garden once the roses are spent. Dogwood and viburnum combine well with azaleas, while ferns and rhododendrons are wonderful companions. Each helps show off the fine qualities of the other.

Plant Collecting

Home gardeners who cultivate theme plants sometimes develop an expertise that grows into a cottage industry. Many of the mail-order catalogs that specialize in one plant group are family businesses that grew out of a plant hobby. Mark Werther—a Philadelphia architect—offers 200 orchid varieties in his catalog. His business began with a few orchids on his windowsill. Several of the miniature rose catalog companies operate out of the owner's suburban backyard. In some cases, the plant business becomes the major source of income. In others, it is a helpful supplement; the fun and challenge are the primary motivations.

To begin building a plant collection—or designing a plant theme garden—first check to see if there are any specialist growers in your area. In recent years, the number of small businesses specializing in daylilies, irises, and azaleas has mushroomed. It may be possible to locate all the plant varieties you need right on your own doorstep, rather than purchasing them by mail from distant destinations, where the plant size will probably be smaller than what a local grower can supply.

You may also want to join a specialist plant society to learn more about your interest. A local botanical garden or horticultural society will be able to supply you with addresses for dozens of plant societies, such as the American Pentstemon Society and the American Boxwood Society. These plant societies publish newsletters with the names of mail-order suppliers, so if you cannot find a good local source for your plant specialty, begin building up a collection by mail. Newsletters also provide the opportunity to correspond with other members and to swap plants.

Hybrids and Heirloom Plants

Hybridizing has expanded the choice of plants in many categories. Out of 30,000 orchid species, hybridizers have developed more than 100,000 varieties, and the work continues. The Dutch have developed perennial tulips that will come back each year with vigor, and new daffodil hybrids are introduced regularly.

While working to develop new flower forms and colors,

hybridizers also hope to improve the general qualities of the plant, perhaps extending its season or increasing its hardiness and disease resistance. In some cases the entire plant family is radically improved. At one time lilies were considered difficult to grow. Then Jan de Graaff, a Dutch hybridizer who emigrated to Oregon, developed a strain of Asiatic lilies named "Mid-Century." They grew vigorously, flowered profusely, propagated easily, and were disease-resistant. Suddenly lilies were as easy to grow as daffodils and could come back year after year. De Graaff developed hundreds of hybrids, dramatically increasing the choice of flower color and form for home gardeners throughout the world.

More recently, Fred Meyer, a bulb breeder working in Escondido, California, has introduced a new alstroemeria (Inca lily) hybrid called the Meyer alstroemeria. It is a cross between evergreen and deciduous species he collected in Chile. Unlike the renowned Ligtu hybrids, which are difficult to grow and propagate, the Meyer alstroemeria will sprout easily from seed; it is also less demanding in its growing requirements. Alstroemeria were once primarily the province of professional cut-flower growers and florists because they were so hard to grow. This new hybrid is expected to transform the bulb into a popular home garden plant in southern California and, when more is known about its hardiness, possibly even farther north.

While some collectors and hybridizers are working to develop new, improved varieties, other collectors are motivated by preservation. An increasing number of people are concerned about the future of native wildflower species. As their habitats are taken over for development, the number of wildflower species is shrinking. Spearheaded by Lady Bird Johnson and others, home gardeners are harvesting seeds and planting them in miniature wildflower preserves.

Antique vegetables and flowers are another popular collection theme. Several catalogs now offer obscure, old-fashioned edible plant varieties that are still worth growing.

At Monticello, Thomas Jefferson's historic garden in Charlottesville, Virginia, curators had to become plant detectives, searching the world for samples of the exact varieties Jefferson once grew. Fortunately, men like Jefferson kept detailed records of their annual plantings, so it has been possible to restore his garden fairly accurately.

Plant Collections in Your Landscape

In addition to being fun to collect, certain plants are valuable for specific landscape uses. Daffodils are excellent meadow flowers and also bloom well in deciduous woods. For an extended bloom display, interplant bearded irises with daylilies. Once the irises finish flowering, the daylilies begin. Dwarf conifers look good in rock gardens, adding height as well as a variety of shapes, colors, and textures to the composition.

Ornamental grasses are enjoying a surge of popularity as people recognize their strong landscape characteristics. Generally a durable, hardy plant, many types of ornamental grasses can be grown in difficult conditions such as exposed windy sites and dry slopes. Available in a wide range of sizes—from a few inches tall, suitable for ground cover, to large specimen varieties that stand higher than 6 feet—they develop decorative long-lasting flower plumes and look sensational planted as a lawn highlight. Ornamental grasses don't need pruning or mowing, many are drought-tolerant, and they add an extra dimension of sound and movement in the garden when breezes rustle their long leaves. In the past, ornamental grasses have been used as accent plants, but innovative designers are now using them as a primary focus as well (see page 19).

Ferns are another large plant family that includes a remarkably wide variety of shapes and sizes. Some are extremely cold-hardy, others are tropical. Some have broad, flat leaves, others unfurl swordlike spikes; many have feathery fronds. They can be tiny plants just a few inches tall or many feet tall, like the Australian tree ferns. Ferns are wonderful around ponds, in woodland gardens, as accents mixed with flowers, and in rock gardens. Collectors in northern states will even grow tender ferns (such as tree ferns) in tubs so they can be used outdoors in summer and taken indoors for protection during winter.

Collecting plants can be a challenging hobby. For some gardeners, the hobby grows into a business; for others, a special group of plants simply becomes the focus of their landscape design. In either case, you will find that deepening your knowledge of a specific plant family, with all its strengths, quirks, and diversity, is a joy.

▲
Large island beds filled with mass plantings of annuals create a garden oasis within a contrasting environment. Regular irrigation makes this garden possible. If you have limited space or strict water constraints, scale down the size of the beds. The straight wooden edging along the axial paths contributes to a somewhat formal look, but the hard lines are softened by the plants spilling over the edges.

▶
It is possible to plant a "ring around the tree" of annuals by thinning a tree to allow the sun to filter through. Combining different flower forms and colors adds to the design interest. Here brilliantly colored spikes of scarlet sage *(Salvia splendens)* are intensified when encircled by soft pink globes of wax begonia *(Begonia semperflorens-cultorum).*

▲
The most dramatic formal annual borders are a masterful combination of color and texture. Here massed "Inca Orange" marigold flowers are contrasted with the silvery gray leaves of "Silver Lace" dusty miller, which also echoes the lacy pattern of the marigold foliage. A narrow strip of salmon-colored geraniums provides a subtle accent.

Traditionally, a cutting garden of annuals is located out of sight of the main garden because heavy picking depletes the floral display. When the blooms are at their peak, however, it is a place of great delight. Make the beds narrow so that all the flowers can be reached easily for cutting, and cover the paths between them with gravel, mulch, or straw to minimize weeds and mud.

Most flowers that are good for cutting crave sunlight. To maximize their exposure, face the bed toward the sun and plant shorter flowers in front so they are not shaded by taller ones. Many annuals make excellent cut flowers. Pictured here are some of the best: marigolds, salvias, stock, snapdragons, geraniums, zinnias, and tall, pink-flowered cleomes.

Several ornamental grasses, such as this fountain grass *(Pennisetum setaceum)*, can be grown as annuals to bloom the first year. Valued in gardens for their beautiful flower plumes and seed heads, they look wonderful either as a background to other plantings or mixed with annuals or perennials.

Impatiens is an excellent choice to plant under trees because it grows well in shade, and its shallow root system won't compete with the deeper roots of the tree. One of the few annuals that blooms in shade, impatiens will also do well in full sun if the soil is kept cool and moist by high humus content. In frost-free climates, impatiens blooms year-round, although it needs to be cut back periodically to keep it from getting leggy.

A bed of annuals is a refreshing change from shrubs, the standard foundation planting. Here tall cleomes are placed in back for height, while the shorter impatiens, "Silver Lace" dusty miller, and wax begonias show off in front. Geraniums with variegated leaves flank the cleomes, adding a midsized height to the design. These bright orange flowers also serve as an accent to the pink and silver color scheme.

Although all annuals need some water during their brief life, a surprising number are fairly drought-tolerant and will grow in poor soil. This wide border features blue and red salvias, zinnias, marigolds, and wax begonias. Other annuals that will live with less water include California poppies, baby's breath, portulacas, statice, gazanias, and alyssum.

Although these annuals will grow under stressful conditions, they per-

form better with ample water and good soil. If there is a water shortage *and* soil is poor, take the time to improve the soil so the plants have to cope with only one stress instead of two. To improve any plant's chance for success, spread bountiful quantities of manure 1 to 2 inches thick and blend with 10 pounds of complete fertilizer and 10 pounds of gypsum for every 100 square feet of garden.

▲
Most perennials bloom for just a few weeks, while annuals continue to flower throughout the growing season. By combining them, the annuals provide season-long splashes of color, while the perennials create a dynamic, changing picture as different plants come into bloom. Here large pink flowers of perennial *Sedum spectabile*, which blooms in late summer and early fall, add exuberance to annual marigolds and begonias.

▲
Annuals generally look best when planted in massed groups. Mix different colors to create a happy, carefree look. Related pinks and blues give a more serene feeling, while yellows, reds, and oranges are a dynamic, energizing combination. Here the gardener has made a bold statement by combining complementary colors; bright yellow marigolds and blue cornflowers.

▲

Low-growing annuals make a delightful edging on perennial beds. Here Livingstone daisies *(Dorotheanus bellidiformis)* soften the transition between a moss-covered stone edge and strappy leaves of agapanthus. Other annuals that have a similar effect are ageratum, alyssum, anchusa, dwarf asters, wax begonias, brachycome, browallia, calendula, candytuft (beware of snails), celosia, dusty miller, forget-me-nots, and pansies.

▲

Annuals are well suited to containers because of their shallow root system. Set one dramatic pot on its own or clump several together to make an attractive group. Design possibilities are endless. Experiment by mixing different annuals within one large container—perhaps with a tall plant in the center, shorter ones around it, and trailing plants at the edge, so they will hang over the sides.

◄

Mix different annuals massed in clumps to create an eye-catching composition. Warm reds and yellows create a sunny effect that is accented by the gray stone and "Silver Lace" dusty miller. The spiky feathers of the plumed celosia also contrast effectively with the round marigold and zinnia flowers, mounded wax begonias, and lacy leaves of dusty miller.

Bulbs are ideal for containers because you can whisk the plants out of sight when they go through their unattractive dying-back stage. Potted bulbs are also a dramatic way to welcome spring without the expense of planting hundreds of them. Pack as many as possible into each pot. A full bouquet in each container is much prettier than a sparse one.

It is not a good idea to mix different kinds of bulbs in the same pot, because they probably will not bloom simultaneously. Instead, for diversity, group pots containing different varieties. Containers are portable, so it's easy to experiment to find the best arrangement.

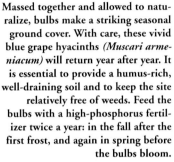

Massed together and allowed to naturalize, bulbs make a striking seasonal ground cover. With care, these vivid blue grape hyacinths *(Muscari armeniacum)* will return year after year. It is essential to provide a humus-rich, well-draining soil and to keep the site relatively free of weeds. Feed the bulbs with a high-phosphorus fertilizer twice a year: in the fall after the first frost, and again in spring before the bulbs bloom.

Planted in clumps by color and type, bulbs look much bolder and more attractive. It is not difficult to create a sophisticated design such as these islands of tulip varieties surrounded by a blue sea of grape hyacinths. The trick is to select bulbs that will bloom simultaneously. Read catalogs and labels to determine whether a bulb is considered an early, mid-season, or late bloomer.

In frost-free climates, where tulips and other bulbs that require chilling are difficult to grow, choose spring-flowering bulbs native to South Africa, the Mediterranean, or Mexico. One possibility is this lavender baboon flower *(Babiana stricta)*, so named because South African baboons eat the corms. Other bulbs for southern climates are freesia, ixia, sparaxis, ipheion, *Scilla campanulata*, and watsonia.

▲

Crown imperial is a spectacular lesser-known bulb that blooms for several weeks in spring. It grows up to 4 feet tall and produces a showy cluster of brightly colored yellow or orange bell-like flowers under a crown of slender, arching leaves. In a landscape this flower is a dramatic accent when grown in clumps with the bulbs planted about 10 inches apart. Because the flowers bloom at the end of a tall, bare stem, they are also especially useful as a background.

Crown imperials grow best planted in dappled shade in moist, humus-rich soil. A woodland environment is ideal. Plant them on their sides because the shallow depression on the top of each bulb can collect water and induce rot. Once planted, they prefer not to be moved. Unfortunately, they do not grow well in the warm-summer regions of the South or in the dry areas of the Southwest.

▼

Native blue phlox (Phlox divaricata) is ideal to combine with tulips. A low-to-the-ground creeping perennial, phlox is an attractive ground cover while the bulbs are coming up, and it helps hide their dying leaves at the end of the season. When they bloom simultaneously, the result is breathtaking.

Other plants that are excellent to combine with bulbs are forget-me-nots, primroses, pansies, and violas. Generally the combination looks better if you plant masses of one color, rather than a busy mixture.

Overplanting bulbs is another way to make a smooth, colorful transition between spring and summer. As soon as annuals are available, plant them between the bulbs. As the bulbs fade and die back, the annuals begin to thrive, masking their unsightly withering leaves with cheerful summer flowers.

◀

The Atamasco lily (Zephyranthes atamasco) is a striking spring-blooming native of the Carolina lowlands. In sandy soil, south of Washington, D.C., it naturalizes freely, seeding itself in sun or partial shade.

▶

Calla lilies are amazingly adaptable perennial bulbs to grow in mild-winter areas. They thrive in soil ranging from dry to moist and will grow in sun or light shade. They have one of the longest bloom seasons of any bulb, lasting for several months starting in early spring. On the East Coast, callas are not reliably hardy north of Charleston, South Carolina, but can easily be grown in a container and moved indoors during winter.

▼

The fall-blooming colchicum, or autumn crocus, is ideal for planting in a lawn (it will bloom through turf) or rock garden to get a splash of late-season color. Like naked ladies (*Amaryllis belladonna*), colchicum flowers bloom on bare stems. The leaves turn yellow and die off, so plant them in informal settings. Despite its common name and resemblance to the true crocus, the autumn crocus is not related.

▲

For an early burst of color even before the snow has completely melted, plant winter aconites and snowdrops. Both plants do well tucked in the crevices of a rock garden or between stepping stones. They are also beautiful in drifts under deciduous trees and shrubs, and are ideal for naturalizing. Do not disturb them once they are planted. To keep a naturalized area weed-free, mulch with shredded leaves.

◀

Dahlias are a wonderful bulb for summer bloom. They range in height from 1-foot-high border plants to tall, shrubby trees up to 16 feet high. The flowers come in many different shapes and colors, and the bloom season lasts for months. In warm climates they can be left in the ground until they become overcrowded and need dividing. In regions where the ground freezes, dig up the tubers and store them in a cool, dry place over winter.

Daffodils, the most loved of all bulbs, are like old friends, returning year after year and often surviving total neglect. Some of the daffodils planted 200 years ago in Virginia gardens are still blooming. Here clumps of daffodils planted in a Pennsylvania meadow bloom more profusely each spring as the bulbs multiply and increase in strength. To encourage naturalizing, plant daffodils in humus-rich soil and feed them with superphosphate (an economical substitute for bonemeal bulb fertilizer), twice a year, in early spring before flowering and again in autumn, after the last frost.

Daffodils are ideal to grow in the light shade of deciduous woods because they bloom before the new spring leaves have formed a dense canopy. During the hot summer months, shade is an asset to the bulbs, because it keeps the soil cool. Plant the woods with drifts and clumps of daffodils, such as this cluster of dwarf "Tête-a-Tête" flowers, and they will naturalize and multiply each year.

Unlike tulips, which are not strong enough to push up through sod, daffodils will grow aggressively in lawns. Plant islands of color in your lawn like Claude Monet's clump of "Professor Einstein" shown here, or allow drifts of flowers to flow like a river through the grass.

To plant, use a lawn edger to cut strips of turf to a depth of 3 inches so the sod can be peeled back to reveal bare soil. After planting the bulbs, simply roll back the turf. Since the dying leaves return energy to the bulb, they should not be mowed until they are completely spent, usually 2 or 3 months after flowering.

Daylilies are well loved for their adaptability, long bloom season, easy care requirements (just bait for snails in spring when the new growth appears), and breathtaking variety of beautiful flower colors. Although each flower lasts only a day, the plant produces new flowers throughout its blooming period.

There are thousands of daylily hybrids to choose from. Some bloom early (late May and June), some midseason (July), and others not until August and September. For a dramatic flower display such as this, plant massed clumps of different varieties from each bloom season. Before choosing your favorites, find out which hybrids do best in your region.

The wild daylily known as "wayside" is a hardy plant, indigenous to China and Japan. It has a simpler flower form than the hybridized varieties and looks delicate and natural in any informal setting. Because this daylily requires little maintenance, it is also an excellent choice to use on steep slopes to help retain the soil.

Daylilies are excellent to mass along a sunny walkway because their fountaining foliage softens the edge of the path without impinging on walking space. Here evergreen shrubs are interplanted among the daylilies to provide an attractive border in winter when the daylilies have died back. There are also cold-tender varieties that remain green throughout the year and do well in southern California and the Deep South.

In recent years daylily hybridizers have introduced dwarf varieties that grow only 2 feet high, instead of the usual 3 or 4. "Stella d'Oro," shown here, is particularly popular because it is a compact, vigorous perennial with long-lasting blooms, ideal for small spaces. It will grow reliably in zones 4 to 10.

◄

The fern family is large and diverse both in range of hardiness and in appearance. In this exquisite tropical water garden, a wide variety of ferns have been combined to create a lush composition. For this effect, mix ferns with different leaf textures, such as the arching, feathery fronds of the Australian tree fern, the soft, round leaves of the maidenhair spleenwort on the rocks, and the long, spiky leaves of Japanese silver fern.

▼

Ferns also mix well with flowers. Interplant a clump of ferns, such as this hardy Pennsylvania-native ostrich fern *(Matteuccia struthiopteris)*, with spring-flowering bulbs. Both the ostrich fern and the Spanish bluebells *(Endymion hispanicus)* shown here prefer partial shade and plenty of moisture. Later in the season, the fern will hide the dying bulb leaves.

►

Australian tree ferns *(Cyathea australis)* eventually grow as tall as small trees, and their feathery fronds create a wonderful canopy. Several planted together make an unusual tropical forest. Use their shade to underplant with sun-tender plants, such as these cymbidiums, and their trunks to host epiphytic plants that don't need soil, such as the staghorn fern. Allow baby's tears *(Soleirolia)* to grow and spread for a lush forest floor.

▲

Because of their shallow root systems, ferns are well suited for shady rock gardens. Here mounds of maidenhair ferns *(Adiantum pedatum)* echo the round shapes of moss-covered boulders. Experiment with different ferns, keeping in mind their fascinating diverse foliage textures.

For people who cannot bend to the ground to till a garden, or simply prefer not to, these raised beds are the perfect solution. Wide brick paths make the garden accessible by wheelchair, and the rim on each box makes a convenient seat. Raised planters are also perfect for gardening on a paved surface, such as a city or roof garden.

Many of the most useful herbs do very well in containers. Use potted herbs to create a changeable tableau, such as this lovely grouping around a fountain. Keep a pot of basil or thyme near the kitchen door for easy snipping, and plant mint in a pot, even when buried in the ground, to contain its invasive roots. Potted winter-tender herbs can be moved indoors during the frosted months.

Solve the problem of poor soil by creating slightly raised beds of improved soil for shallow-rooted herbs. Instead of symmetrical rectangles or pie wedges, form beds in an eclectic mix of triangles, trapezoids, and parallelograms floated among flagstone paths. A design such as this is an excellent complement to a modern house with angular lines.

Create a formal herb garden by keeping the lines simple, symmetrical, and clean. Here, a very controlled design has been created in a narrow space. Square beds at one end are varied with triangular beds surrounding a circle at the other end. To maintain the simple design, the herbs are planted in patterns so that the beds mirror each other. A classical-style white marble sculpture enhances the formal feeling.

A strong design is often necessary to give an herb garden a distinctive look, since many useful herbs do not produce showy flowers. Here, a Victorian-style herb garden is created with appropriate accessories: an English hare made of lead, placed at the center of a circular herb garden, and an ornate cast-iron bench, which picks up the color of the lead hare. A pair of ornamental urns reinforce the Victorian feeling.

A woven basket bee skep is a lovely accent in an herb garden that has been used since medieval times. Bees are always useful in a garden because they improve pollination, but whether you cultivate a hive in your skep or not, it will make a marvelous ornament. Several specialist herb catalogs offer these by mail. You might also consider having your skep shellacked to make it weather-resistant.

Sixteenth-century Elizabethans mastered the art of knotted herb gardens. Plant bands of contrasting herbs and shrubs in patterns that can be pruned to appear as though they were passing over and under each other. Herbs and shrubs that lend themselves to this use are germander, rosemary, thyme, dwarf lavender, lavender cotton *(Santolina chamaecyparissus)*, and boxwood. Fill the spaces between the knotted strands with other plants, flowers, or colored pebbles and gravel.

▼

One way to create an unusual herb garden is to use striking contrasts in scale and texture. Here a dramatic contrast of scale is achieved with high hedges of hemlock *(Tsuga canadensis)* planted around a sunken herb garden, where the herbs are allowed to spill.

▼

In a formal herb garden plants are often grouped according to traditional usage—medicinal herbs, dye plants, and culinary herbs, for example. To enliven a formal herb garden, plant some species known for colorful flowers, such as foxgloves, bee balm, and chives. Here, clumps of flowering African daisy, *(Pyrethrum roseum)* decorate the garden. The petals of this plant also produce an effective insecticide called pyrethrum.

▼

Create a fragrant walkway by planting chamomile, thyme, and other scented low-growing plants between the cracks of broken flagstone. In this garden the surrounding borders and beds also have their own themes. A wattle fence and a unicorn sculpture placed in one of the beds help evoke a medieval feeling.

◄

A garden seat in the midst of an herb garden is a wonderful way to enjoy the scent of fresh herbs. Thyme growing at the base of this bench sends its pleasant perfume into the air when stepped on. The famous British writer and gardener Vita Sackville-West even designed a stone seat overgrown with chamomile *(Anthemis nobilis)* in her Sissinghurst garden. Chamomile releases its scent when crushed and is tough enough to sit on.

▲
Some herbs, such as this brilliant English lavender (Lavandula angusti-folia), can be used in massed plantings to create a colorful border, hedge, or edging. Claude Monet combined bright purple lavender with a sea green bench for a striking effect. The curve of the bench is repeated in the lavender planting, increasing the sense of harmony.

◄
Use the bright pink, fragrant flowers of creeping thyme "Annie Hall" to fill in the gaps between paving stones. Woolly thyme (Thymus pseudo-lanuginosus) also hugs the ground, never growing above 3 inches, and has tiny, gray-green furry leaves. For an applelike scent, use chamomile.

Named after Iris, the Greek goddess of the rainbow, bearded irises come in every color combination imaginable, including black, and make excellent color accents. Most have an extended bloom season and, depending on the variety, will flower beginning in early spring until summer. Heights vary from 8 to 27 inches. Remontant, or reblooming, iris will bloom a second time at Christmas in warm climates, such as coastal California.

Yellow flag *(Iris pseudacorus)* thrives in shallow water. Plant it beside a stream or pond in full to light shade. The bright yellow blossoms grow on tall stalks up to 5 feet high and will rebloom every year. Under favorable conditions, the plant will self-sow prolifically, making large colonies.

Siberian irises will naturalize into profusely blooming tight clumps that rarely need dividing. Plant them in drifts in a natural setting or in a perennial border for cut flowers. They are easy to grow, adaptable to many climates, and tolerate both wet and dry soil.

Japanese irises *(Iris ensata)* a showy flat-flowered species, make extraordinary indoor floral arrangements. They prefer lots of moisture when actively growing, but will withstand drought at other times of the year. White, blue, lavender, pink, and purple flower varieties are all dramatic additions to the landscape or lovely in a cutting garden.

▲
Lilies are excellent flowers to use as a highlight in a perennial border. Even one stem, in full bloom, is an eye-catching feature. Place the plant where the striking flower form and colors can be seen and appreciated in detail. Pictured here is *Lilium* "Imperial Crimson."

▲
Lilies have a reputation for being difficult to grow, but most of the almost 80 species are in fact easy to care for if they are grown under the right conditions. Requirements vary widely depending on the species, so it is important to learn the proper care of each specific plant. The erect-facing "Mid-Century" hybrid shown here will naturalize if planted in a shady spot with well-drained, humus-rich soil, such as this woodland grove.

◄
Popular with florists because of their sweet fragrance, long stems, and long-lasting beauty, lilies are a wonderful addition to a cutting garden. Here the white blooms of the summer-flowering Madonna lilies *(Lilium candidum)* also provide a dramatic contrast to the adjacent blood-red roses and, in the distance, the arid landscape.

▶ Cymbidiums, which can be grown outdoors in subtropical regions, are ideal container plants since they flourish when root-bound. If you wish, keep the leafy plants out of sight in filtered shade until they produce their showy flowers in winter. (They won't bloom unless they get cool nights in late summer and fall.)

After they bloom, put them in a prominent spot, bait for snails, and, if desired, cut a few bloom spikes to enjoy inside.

Depending on the hybrid, cymbidiums bloom from November to May. Collect a variety of types for different flower colors and bloom times.

▼ Orchids are divided into two main categories: terrestrials, which grow in soil, and epiphytes, which grow on trees or rocks and obtain their nourishment through their leaves and aerial roots. In a tropical rock garden, combine shallow-rooted terrestrial orchids and epiphytes for an unusual display of exotic-looking flowers.

◀ Many of the terrestrial orchids, such as the paphiopedilums, make unusual, very effective hanging-basket arrangements. Paphiopedilums are cold-tender, suffering if temperatures drop below 60 degrees. Choose different varieties for bloom times in all four seasons. Keep them in shade during the summer.

▶

A mature clump of dormant eulalia *(Miscanthus sinensis)*, growing up to 6 feet tall, is a striking feature in a winter landscape. Plant this ornamental grass as a background to a perennial border, as a specimen to highlight a particular spot in the garden, or as a contrast to low-growing ground covers. The feathery panicles, or seed heads, are also excellent to use in long-lasting dried arrangements.

▼

Gracefully arching leaves, a tall, mounding form, and spiky pink or mauve panicles make the annual fountain grass *(Pennisetum setaceum)* a popular addition in flower beds. Here, in the center of a bed of brightly colored wax begonias, the green grassy leaves intensify the red of the begonia flowers.

Use ornamental grasses to break monotony in an area planted with ground cover. Here the silvery blue foliage of the upright blue fescue grass *(Festuca ovina,* "glauca") blends effectively with the leaf color of the stonecrop *(Sedum spurium)* ground cover, but provides a pleasing contrast in size, form, and texture.

▲

◀

The beauty of perennial ornamental grasses is that they provide year-round interest and they change with the seasons. In spring, the growth is fresh and deep green. By summer the attractive flower and seed heads develop. Then, in autumn, the grasses begin to dry and turn such colors as gold, russet, and pale green, as shown here. In winter their forms are beautifully accented in a stark landscape. To appreciate the wide variety of ornamental grasses available, plant a varied collection.

▶ Easy to grow, adaptable, and versatile in a landscape, ornamental grasses can be a sophisticated addition to a floral border. The play of light on their translucent panicles, their undulating motion, and the rustling sound they make when disturbed by breezes add powerful elements even to a formal design. In this border a pleasing balance is achieved by successfully mixing heights, forms, and colors.

◀ The gently drooping fountain form of many of the ornamental grasses has a softening effect in a garden. To blur the edge of a path, or to soften hard lines, plant a border of grass such as this handsome fountain grass *(Pennisetum alopecuroides)*. In the wind the long leaves will move in gentle ripples of silver and gold, depending on the season.

▲ Ornamental grasses can be used in both formal and informal settings. In a large informal flower border, tall varieties work well as backgrounds to smaller plants. Since they require very little maintenance, they are a good choice for hard-to-reach spots.

▶ Ornamental grasses provide an ideal natural transition between land and water. Their arching forms hang over the water and create interesting reflections. But bear in mind the size of the pond. The bulky molinia grass shown here is in perfect scale to its surroundings. For a smaller pond, consider a low-growing grass that grows in little clumps, such as blue fescue.

Peonies come in two types: herbaceous and tree. The herbaceous plants need a sharp winter to grow and bloom, and they die back each fall. Tree peonies grow as woody, deciduous shrubs up to 4 feet tall and should not be cut back in winter; they do not need cold to bloom, so some varieties can grow in the South. The spectacular pink and white double blooms of this herbaceous peony and pink spiky foxglove blossoms make a particularly pleasing combination. Another good pair is peony "Ivory Jewel" and Siberian iris, which also bloom simultaneously.

Named after a famous British plant explorer who discovered it in China, this tree peony, "Joseph Rock" *(Paeonia suffruticosa)*, is among the rarest and most expensive. All existing specimens in this country were propagated from the one he found. Collectors are willing to pay as much as $100 for one root of the vigorous shrub that produces these striking creamy white flowers with maroon throats.

A long driveway lined with peonies lifts the mundane to the lovely. Tree peonies *(Paeonia suffruticosa)* are a good choice because their bushy form will remain tidy, and their huge, brightly colored blossoms make a dramatic first impression. The plants will thrive in sun or partial shade and, when mature, will bear 50 or more blooms. Here a row of deep red "Thunderbolt" and yellow "Amber Moon" tree peonies are a welcome view for drivers.

Although tree peonies are expensive, they are a worthwhile investment because they produce a profusion of large dramatic flowers in spring.

▶

Create a soft, fresh look with a spring-blooming border of perennials that produce blue flowers. Here pale blue phlox *(Phlox divaricata)*, mid-blue Jacob's-ladder *(Polemonium)*, and dark blue ajuga accented with yellow alyssum *(Aurinia saxatilis)* and pink azaleas are a beautiful herald of spring. In a few months, the daylilies behind will take center stage with their summer flowers.

▼

Popularized by English garden designer and writer Gertrude Jekyll at the turn of this century, the classic perennial border is generally backed by a wall or dark green hedge. The challenge when designing a border is to choose plants that create a beautiful combination of patterns, colors, and textures, and to see that different plants will become prominent as the seasons progress. In this late-spring border, pale blue phlox, white deutzia, and blue Siberian iris dominate. Come summer, other flowers will take over the show.

▲

Plant a sunny, summer-blooming perennial border with plants that bloom in the warm color spectrum—shades of yellow, gold, red, and pink. Here islands of red Flanders poppies, magenta catchfly or campion (Silene), misty white baby's breath (Gypsophilia elegans), and blue larkspur float among a sea of yellow coreopsis and yarrow. Silvery lamb's ears foliage is an eye-catching accent.

▲

Choose from a wide selection of fall-blooming perennials to make a varied display later in the season. Some good choices are shown here. They include everlasting *(Helichrysum)*, which produces pearly white flowers; obedient plant *(Physostegia virginiana)*, so named because its tubular pink-purple flowers will stay wherever they are placed; lavender New England asters; pink Japanese anemones; and white boltonia.

▶

Mass-plant perennial flowers to create a drift effect. Here *Rudbeckia fulgida* "Goldsturm" and purple coneflowers *(Echinacea)* provide a colorful, naturalistic swath of bloom along the side of a house.

▲

Some flowers, such as these perennial Oriental poppies, take on a new dimension when their translucent petals are backlighted by the sun. For a particularly sophisticated aesthetic effect, plant a bed that will benefit from light coming from different angles throughout the day.

▶

Plant a show-stopping street-front display of annuals and perennials by interplanting different varieties. If necessary, choose plants that remain fairly low, as shown here, so they won't block the view from the porch. This vibrant blend of colors and textures mixes pink *Sedum spectabile* with golden French marigolds and gloriosa daisies, blood-red snapdragons, white mums and sweet alyssum, and silvery leafed artemesia.

Use flowering perennial vines, such as this clematis "Ernest Markham," to add height to a flower bed and to soften a solid wall. Let the colors in the wall, such as this red brick, influence your palette. Here pink foxgloves, pale lavender bearded irises, scarlet peonies, and magenta clematis create a harmonious composition.

Instead of a blooming perennial border, create a leafy emphasis by intermixing hostas with different leaf colors and forms. Hostas are excellent for low-maintenance gardens: they are easy to grow and do well even in deep shade. Use them as a ground cover or as a foundation planting (see pages 159 and 173).

Put very tall perennials in the back of a bed, with shorter ones in front, to create a sloping hillside effect that's in proper scale to large surroundings. Here the lanky yellow verbascum in the background is in proportion to the depth of the bed and the sweep of the land behind. The plants gradually become shorter as they move toward the front, with blue bellflowers *(Campanula)* and pink yarrow slightly lower than the verbascum, fronted by yellow and red Asiatic lilies, orange cosmos, and pale blue phlox. Dianthus "Scarlet Charm" and annual pink candytuft make a colorful edging. By the time these spring flowers fade, other summer-blooming perennials in the bed will dominate.

◄ Flank a walkway with parallel perennial borders for a dramatic, opulent floral display. These late-spring/early-summer borders feature silver lamb's ears, pale pink evening primrose, yellow coreopsis, and white perennial salvia on the left, and an edging of pink verbena and white pansies on the right.

◄ Use perennials to create the informal exuberance of an English cottage garden by allowing the plants to spill onto a path. Here a mixture of perennials and annuals chosen for their contrasting foliage and flowers transforms a straight brick walkway into a meandering trail.

▲ An effective perennial bed doesn't have to be a complicated mix or include hard-to-find plants. Here the fairly simple combination of tall yellow verbascum "Silver Candelabra" contrasting with lower-growing rose-pink campion *(Silene)* makes an interesting, very pretty display.

▶ By the sea, where the soil is sandy with a touch of salt and the winds can be strong, choose perennials that will withstand these special conditions. Shown here in the autumn are yellow coreopsis, pink chrysanthemums, red dragon's blood, and yellow black-eyed Susans *(Rudbeckia)*.

Pillar training is a dramatic way to show off a climbing rose and saves space in a small garden. Here a picture window view of rolling lawns was created by training a climbing rose called "American Pillar" to grow up and across a wooden frame.

Miniature roses are natural dwarf forms of their full-size relatives and require the same care and maintenance. Their diminutive size makes them ideal for small gardens. Depending on whether they are upright or trailing, they can be used as small specimens or massed to create a low border or ground cover. Here the popular white-flowering hybrid "Popcorn" has been trained as a potted tree.

Roses are magnificent in either formal or informal settings. You need not plant a "rose garden" to enjoy them. Here a brilliant red, small climbing rose is a perfect single specimen on a white picket fence.

Old rose varieties have been known to thrive for decades on abandoned homesites or in neglected cemeteries. Many are known for their sweet scent and generally have a more billowing form than modern roses. They can be used not only as landscape specimens, but also as hedges, climbers, and ground covers. Due to an increase in their popularity, mail-order companies now offer a large selection of old rose varieties.

In North America, tree roses are generally created from upright-growing rose varieties and are used in formal settings. Here, in Claude Monet's garden in Giverny, France, a weeping rose variety creates a cascading tree form that looks at home in a relaxed bed of orange daylilies. As the season progresses, the rose canes will be pruned before they reach the ground.

Climbing roses take up little space and add color and drama to a garden. Look for places where you might squeeze in a climbing rose near a flowering shrub, such as this hydrangea. The combination of large lavender-pink hydrangea blossoms and small bright pink roses is especially effective.

Old-fashioned roses are regaining popularity as more people discover their winsome qualities and natural strengths. They are often hardier, more disease-resistant, and even sweeter-smelling than their modern cousins. One of the most popular is "La Reine Victoria," prized for its intense fragrance and profuse, long-lasting repeat blooms that look exquisite in floral arrangements.

To show off your roses, display them against a uniform dark background. In this formal rose garden, a yew hedge serves as an excellent backdrop and also forms the walls of a square garden room. Several rose varieties planted in linear beds, plain brick paving, and a classical urn planted with a single dracaena, all contribute to the formality of the design.

▲
Use evergreen shrubs and trees to provide year-round interest in a garden. Many landscape architects believe that a Japanese garden should contain at least 75 percent evergreens. In this remarkable Japanese-style garden in Pennsylvania, evergreen plants include a pachysandra ground cover, spreading juniper, Korean boxwood, evergreen azaleas, weeping hemlock, weeping spruce, and Japanese cedar *(Cryptomeria japonica)*.

▶
Blend different varieties of trees and shrubs, with varying colors and textures, to create a "tapestry garden." Here the young spring foliage of a red maple, silver-leafed weeping pear, and "Aureum" maple, with its bright yellow leaves that will turn pale green in summer, combine to form an especially impressive design.

▶

The California-native Matilija poppy *(Romneya coulteri)* is a splendid, drought-tolerant landscape plant for warm-climate gardens. Feathery flowers resembling fried eggs bloom from midspring through summer. The 6-foot-tall shrubs require full sun and some space to spread *(the plant can become invasive)*, but little other care. Use these plants as specimen shrubs, as shown here, or on a hillside for erosion control.

To add structure to a border design, mix blooming shrubs with annuals and perennials. Here the early summer-blooming *Spiraea nipponica* "Snowmound," which will eventually grow to 8 feet, is planted with peonies, bearded irises, and a pink gas plant *(Dictamnus albus)*. Other flowering shrubs that are an asset in a border with perennials include roses, hydrangeas, azaleas, potentillas, and in temperate climates, lantanas, camellias, and abutilons. Consider bloom times as you make your choices.

You don't need acres of land to plant an orchard. Apples and other deciduous fruit trees, can be espaliered to grow along a wire fence. It takes many years to achieve a "Belgian fence," as pictured here, but your effort and patience will be rewarded with a striking hedge as well as a bountiful harvest.

Clematis, shown here growing with a climbing rose, are beautiful, undemanding vines that are happiest when their roots are cool (plant them deep and provide mulch) and their tops are in the sun. Be sure that the soil is neither too acidic nor too alkaline. Among the 200-odd species (and hundreds more hybrids), some are hardy, others less so. Bloom time, blossom color, and form vary by species or hybrid, but there is a clematis that will flower in almost every month. Choose the type that best suits your needs.

Dwarf conifers come in a range of colors, heights, forms, and needle types, and are valuable plants, especially for small spaces. Combine different varieties to showcase their diversity, or select one or two as highlights in your landscape. Plant them in a low-growing rock garden to add height, or on an inaccessible hillside since they don't require a lot of care. For shady areas, choose conifers from among the fir, yew, cedar, and hemlock families.

Boxwood is a popular shrub for creating the geometric patterns of parteres—garden beds outlined by a low-growing hedge. The seventeenth-century French, who had a passion for symmetry, logic, and control over nature used boxwoods extensively. They were planted on a grand scale at châteaux, villas, and castles. The parterre concept crossed the channel to England and was then transplanted to Colonial America, where parterres were planted on both a grand and a modest scale.

The look is as compelling today as it was then and can be scaled down to fit even a tiny garden. Ring a tree or frame a flower bed or herb garden with a parterre of boxwood. Consider creating a repeating, interconnected diamond pattern along a border, and fill in the spaces with blooming annuals. To minimize pruning, use dwarf varieties of boxwood.

Tolerant of both sun and shade, boxwood is popular for topiary. Even a simple balled shape adds a formal, stylized look to walkways and borders. Boxwood is naturally slow-growing so it usually requires pruning only once a year (in late summer) to maintain a tidy outline.

Left unpruned, boxwood grows in a soft, billowing form and is an excellent partition to create garden rooms. Depending on the variety, it remains as small as 3 feet tall or grows as high as 15. English or common boxwood *(Buxus sempervirens)*, which is tall and has a delightful peppery scent, is sensitive to hot summers as well as insects and disease. English boxwood is easiest to grow in the mid-South and Northwest, although gardeners use it throughout North America. Visit local nurseries and botanical gardens to learn the best type of boxwood for your climate and landscape needs.

Camellias are the queen of winter. Together with azaleas, they bring color and variety to gardens as early as September in southern climates. If grown in protected areas, they remain reliably hardy as far north as zone 7. Since they adapt well to containers, camellias can also be grown in cool greenhouses or as flowering house-plants in regions with severe frost.

▼

Camellias were introduced from their native Asia to Europe in the early 1700s, but it was not until 1820 that Richard Rawes, a British sea captain, introduced the first hybrid to Europe. This camellia, named "Captain Rawes" , is one of the largest and most beautiful of all camellias. Today gardeners can choose among hundreds of camellia hybrids, which offer a wide choice of bloom seasons, forms, and colors.

Camellias have been used in Japanese gardens for centuries, where they are cherished for their beauty. Fallen camellia blossoms look like pretty pink confetti, adding a transient beauty to this composition of herons resting among strawberry geraniums *(Saxifraga stolonifera)*. Once camellia petals turn brown, however, they should be raked away because they may harbor petal blight, a stubborn plant disease.

▶

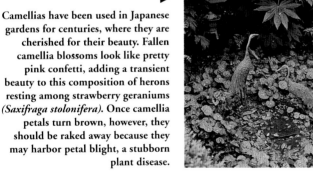

▶

An evergreen shrub that requires shade, camellias are ideal for woodland environments in warm, southern climates and all along the West Coast. Although generally thought of as small shrubs, very old plants will grow as tall as 20 feet. Mix varieties to extend the bloom season from September *(*with sasanquas*)* to late spring *(*with japonicas*)*.

▼
These azaleas have been planted on a berm, or raised ridge of soil, so they will screen the garden from an unattractive neighboring view. In addition to creating a private space in the garden, the berm serves as a display canvas, showing the various jewel-like azalea flowers to best advantage.

►
Azaleas and rhododendrons are both members of a large family of shrubby plants collectively called *Rhododendron*. However, rhododendrons with small leaves and a dense covering of star-shaped flowers are generally called azaleas and tend to be easier to grow because they tolerate heat and drought more successfully. Azaleas look spectacular planted under a dogwood tree. Choose varieties that bloom at the same time.

▲
The classic combination of rhododendron and viburnum makes a delightful contrast in leaf and flower form. The white petals of the Doublefile viburnum *(Viburnum plicatum tomentosum)* intensify the bright red blooms of the rhododendron.

◄
Azaleas relish moist, slightly acid, humus-rich, well-drained soil and are ideal for woodland settings, where they produce vibrant displays of color from early to late spring. Mix varieties with different flowering times for several months of continuous bloom. For added drama, plant a "river" of low-growing spring bulbs such as these Spanish bluebells *(Endymion hispanicus)* and allow them to naturalize around the other woodland plantings.

Left unpruned, as they are here, azaleas will grow in an attractive, free-form shape. For a more formal look, as well as more abundant blooms, shear the bushes each year immediately after they have finished flowering. Like yew and other hedge plants, azaleas can be shaped into balls, boxes, or any form you like.

▲

In a traditional vegetable garden, the plants are arranged in rows with spaces between to allow access for picking, irrigating, and weeding. Surface the paths dividing the rows with a material that will help reduce weeds and mud. Pictured here are grass, beige gravel, and bark paths, each with a different look. Excellent organic materials for covering paths include straw, shredded leaves, and pine needles.

◀

A collection of "square foot" vegetable beds creates a patchwork effect of different leaf textures and colors. Popularized by Mel Bartholomew in his book *Square Foot Gardening* (Rodale Press), the system allows you to conserve water, soil, and labor and is especially ideal for vegetables that grow in a compact area, such as head lettuce, beets, carrots, turnips, and onions.

▲

Train spreading or vining vegetables to grow up on trellises and other supports to create a space-saving vertical garden, or, for variety, grow a few vertical vegetables, such as beans and peas.

◀

Unlike oil and water, flowers and vegetables do mix—with great success. For an ornamental fence around your vegetable plot, plant a row of tall-growing flowers such as trumpet lilies or use them as an accent within a vegetable patch, as shown here. Note the way the crimson snapdragon in the foreground emphasizes the red stalks and veins of the "Ruby" Swiss chard.

◀

Arranged like a traditional herb garden with a sundial in the middle and a fence enclosing the space, this vegetable garden is both ornamental and functional. Contained, raised beds give order to the garden, while the wide space between the beds allows plenty of room for a healthy zucchini to grow beyond its bounds. For pest control and beauty, plant a border of marigolds.

◀

Most vegetables need at least 7 hours of sun a day to produce a bountiful crop. To give your vegetables as much exposure as possible, plant them in rows facing south with the tallest plants to the north, so they do not shade the shorter ones. This old-fashioned Colonial-style vegetable garden includes broom corn (rear) and tobacco (center). Pumpkin vines trail along the ground.

▲

For an unexpected twist, include vegetables in flower beds. Here a mounding zucchini becomes one of the squares in the grid-patterned design, which is echoed in the open squares in the fence beyond. The flowering plants shown here include pink dwarf hollyhocks, rose-pink geraniums, red nasturtiums, white carnations, and yellow marigolds.

Most vegetable gardens need an enclosure, such as this stone and wood fencing, to keep out deer and other foraging animals. You may also take action to prevent damage from intruders on a smaller scale. Studies have shown that French marigolds repel nematodes, microscopic worms that attack plant roots. Interplant vegetables with French marigolds as an attractive, beneficial companion, as shown here.

▼

Many vegetables are attractive enough on their own to merit use as land-scape plants. Curly green parsley, for instance, adds lovely color and texture beside these red zinnias and white vinca, while willowy green tarragon decorates the end of the border.

A beautiful blend of leaf color and form is created by planting silvery green artichokes next to rich red "Ruby" Swiss chard, proving that a vegetable garden can be a visual as well as a culinary feast. Mexican sunflower makes a decorative tall background, while low, spreading white vinca edges the garden.

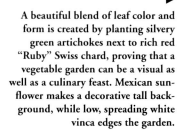

Where soil and drainage are poor, create slightly raised beds by adding improved soil to the site. Then plant a low-growing border, such as this one of creeping thyme, to prevent the beds from washing away. Harvesting is more convenient if you locate your vegetable garden near the kitchen, and damage from animals less likely if you fence in the plot.

Extend the fresh vegetable season by planting frost-hardy crops such as kale, onions, carrots, beets, turnips, brussels sprouts, chard, leeks, and parsley. This clump of ornamental kale is a welcome splash of color in the snow and tasty enough to enjoy eating as well.

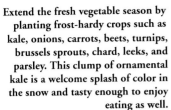

Even without a garden, it's possible to grow vegetables. Tomatoes and peppers are especially good to grow in containers, though tomatoes should be the compact "determinate" type. "Indeterminate" kinds generally grow too tall and top heavy. Here the slicing tomato "Basket King" is attractive in a hanging basket. Among the tomato varieties that adapt well to containers are "Whippersnapper," "Pixie Hybrid," "Tiny Tim," "Salad Top," "Small Fry," "Presto Hybrid," "Gardener's Delight," "Toy Boy," "Sugar Lump," "Tumblin' Tom," and "Stakeless."

Create a hanging salad by planting "Salad Bowl" lettuce in a wire basket lined with sphagnum moss and filled with potting soil. Vegetables in hanging baskets should be watered once a day or more often if the weather is particularly dry or windy.

The vigorous summer-blooming lotus *(Nelumbo nucifera)* will spread and cover a pond to the point of choking if it is not confined. In spring, plant the roots horizontally 4 inches deep in a container, then put the container in the pond with 8 to 12 inches of water over the soil surface. The roots are not hardy below 45° F.

Because water lilies come in bold colors and are relatively large, they are effective from a distance. But be sure to create a setting where the subtleties of petal colors, as well as possible amphibian visitors such as toads and turtles, can be seen up close. There are both tropical and hardy varieties of water lilies. Choose ones that are hardy in your region.

Wealth is no longer a criterion for affording a water garden. With new building techniques and materials such as sheets of PVC or fiberglass forms as a lining, a pond can be built on a very small scale at modest cost. If you plan to grow blooming water plants, choose a spot that gets at least 6 hours of full sun a day. Plant your choices in containers covered with chicken wire to protect them from muskrats, geese, and ducks.

Water plants come in three basic types: submerged varieties, such as watercress and duckweed; floating leaved varieties, such as water lilies; and emergent varieties or bog plants that have only their roots in water. This large pond is planted with some of each type. Among the emergent water plants are the flowering water cannas, bullrushes, and irises with variegated leaves that provide color interest in and out of bloom. Even in a much smaller pond, it's possible to use a wide variety of water plants. Here ornamental grasses, including *Miscanthus sinensis* and mondo grass *(Liriope)*, cascade into the pond, softening the edges.

▲
A meadow of wildflowers will succeed best if the flowers are indigenous, or at least well adapted, to your region. When choosing a wildflower mix, be sure the seeds are for plants that do well in your climate and soil type. Here Texas lupines, called bluebonnets *(Lupinus texensis)*, and Indian paintbrush *(Castilleja indivisa)* thrive in their native Texas, where the soil is alkaline and the winters mild.

▶
As an act of preservation, the South African town of Clanwilliam has devoted 20 acres of semidesert to a garden planted entirely with local wildflowers. These drought-tolerant Namaqualand daisies produce a colorful display of white and yellow flowers during the arid season. These flowers will do especially well in the southwestern region of North America, where the climate is similar to South Africa.

▲
In his novel *East of Eden*, John Steinbeck wrote of California poppies, "if pure gold were liquid and could raise a cream, that golden cream might be the color of the poppies." In their native range, poppies flower from late winter through spring, but with enough water, they can bloom all summer. Since they self-sow freely, they are excellent for naturalizing.

◀

Wildflower aficionados disagree about whether a wildflower garden should contain only wild species or a mixture of wild and cultivated. Purists limit their selection to wild species indigenous to their area. In this rock garden, the owner has limited herself to native North American wildflowers. Pictured are blue *Baptisia australis* (native to Texas) and golden *Lonicera flava* (native to Virginia and other southern states).

◀

Both the bloom and plant forms of many wildflowers, such as this yellow lady's slipper *(Cypripedium calceolus parviflorum)*, are beautifully detailed and intricate. Nevertheless, they can be overlooked in a cluttered setting. To show off diminutive wild plants to their best advantage, plant them in a simple setting where they have a background of ferns or an attractive rock.

◀

When planted in a mass, the dwarf crested iris *(Iris cristata)* makes a lovely spring-blooming ground cover. It is native to the East Coast from Maryland to Georgia. This iris comes in white, light blue, and lilac. Plant it in drifts as a ground cover or as clumps in a rock garden. These irises bloom best in full sun, but will tolerate light shade.

▲

Wildflowers mix admirably with tame, cultivated species. Here delicate scarlet blossoms of wild eastern columbine *(Aquilegia canadensis)*, lavender Jacob's-ladder flowers *(Polemonium caerulea)* in the foreground, and blue annual phlox *(Phlox drummondii)* combine beautifully with daffodils and daylily foliage.

Garden Accents

IN ANY GARDEN there can be two kinds of accents—plant and structural. Plants, or softscape, have an ephemeral quality; hardscape elements such as benches, paths, terraces, fences, and shelters, while also decorative, are more durable or functional. This section deals with hardscape accents. They are as important to the aesthetic success of your garden as the plants themselves, providing focal points in many cases and introducing a human presence to the overall composition.

Use Accents to Establish Style

Many accents—such as paths and fences—perform vital practical functions, but are also highly decorative. Others—such as statues and sundials—are strictly ornamental, and proper placement is the most important consideration. With both utilitarian and decorative garden accents, the challenge is introducing them into the garden in the right scale and the right context. Garden structures can help identify the garden style or theme more quickly than plants alone. A Japanese-style gateway, for example, immediately establishes the concept of an Oriental garden, which is reinforced with stone lanterns, arched footbridges, and compositions using natural boulders. Although the use of appropriate plants—such as bamboo, moss as a ground cover, and azalea shrubs sheared into mounds—helps complete the Oriental look, it generally is not enough to achieve this effect alone without hardscape accents.

An informal English cottage garden, which often relies on a kind of "organized chaos" to be effective, can look like a bewildering jumble without a few vital structures to provide organization: a central brick path with plants spilling into it, a dry wall overflowing with alpine plants and minor bulbs, arbors festooned with flowering vines, a rustic summerhouse or a gazebo

tucked into a corner, and a pitted stone birdbath as a focal point at the center of the garden space or at the termination of a vista. These features, perhaps even more than the plants themselves, are the true hallmarks of an English garden.

Artwork in the Garden

Gardens have long been repositories for art—particularly durable art, such as statuary. The ancient Chinese searched rock falls and river beds for boulders that represented animals—especially mythical animals like dragons—then set them in the garden as focal points. At the other extreme, the Greeks and Romans favored realism, filling their gardens with lifelike statues—heroes, gods, and horses—to symbolize freedom and power. The preference for realism in sculpture was so strong, in fact, that many Mediterranean gardens were actually sculpture gardens rather than plant gardens, with rows of statues placed on pedestals forming avenues and others set in niches within clipped, dark evergreen hedges.

Today, battles rage whenever a sculpture garden is proposed. Proponents on one side prefer sculptures in plain surroundings (as in the Pepsi sculpture garden, in Purchase, New York), while those on the other insist that sculptures be surrounded by beautiful flowering plants (as in Jasmine Hill, near Montgomery, Alabama). In Jasmine Hill, each replica of a Greek marble sculpture is set in a garden specially designed to present it to maximum effect. For example, *Winged Victory*—a headless athletic woman with wings—stands before a reflecting pool surrounded by beds of azaleas and a background of crape myrtle.

There are also disputes among modern sculpture enthusiasts, who regard the garden as the ideal setting for abstract art, and those who feel that a garden should not be filled with unnatural images. The "realists" insist that only harmonious, soothing lines belong in a garden, refusing to admit any harsh lines or reminders of a machine-oriented world into the pastoral setting. Meanwhile, functional tools have found a place in gardens. In rural communities in the midwestern prairie states, it is common to see fences made from old metal wheels strung together, or old hand ploughs set into flower beds and decorated with flowering vines. At Eleutherian Mills, a restored historical garden near Wilmington, Delaware, cogwheels and capstans that were once used in machinery producing gunpowder have been set as lawn accents against ruined walls and planted around with wisteria.

A Place for Contemplation

Since most gardens call for a place to sit quietly and enjoy the surroundings, benches and seats offer some of the most popular accents. A collection of benches may be appropriate if the garden contains many vantage points and vistas, secret spaces, garden rooms, meandering paths, and water features. At Dumbarton Oaks, Washington, D.C., landscape architect Beatrix Farrand installed a vast collection of benches, few of them exactly alike. Some are made of wood, others of stone (mostly concrete or marble), others of metal. Though most of the benches were inspired by English and Italian gardens, the diversity of designs is an appealing feature of the garden.

The same is true of the restored gardens at Colonial Williamsburg, where a vast assortment of Colonial-style bench designs have been used to establish authenticity. One imaginative design features a bench set into the railing of a bridge from which you can view the entire length of the lake. The benches in Williamsburg—almost all made of wood—range in color from brown, cinnamon, and black to cream and white.

In some gardens a distinctive bench design actually becomes a trademark. For example, the Impressionist painter Claude Monet discovered a long, sleek curved bench very much to his liking in a secluded corner of the gardens at Versailles. This unpainted bench was backed against a rough stone wall, with sufficient room for up to six people to sit comfortably and admire the flower garden. Monet copied the design exactly, but painted his version in apple green to match the shutters of the house. In one area of Monet's garden in Giverny, France, three of these benches face each other within a secluded gravel circle. The bench is so distinctive that it has become famous as "Monet's bench," and replicas now appear in other gardens.

However beautiful and tastefully constructed it may be, a bench will flop if it is poorly placed. Writing about the subject in his 1936 book *Garden Decoration and Ornament*, G. A. Jellicoe said, "The first object of a seat is invitation. Its position should be such that it should attract, whether because it offers rest at the end of a long walk, or because it is so placed that its surroundings may give rise to pleasant contemplation. The permanent seat should have a suggestion of background because the human being finds it more restful and comforting to have a sense of shelter and to look towards one direction only."

Water Features

A water feature is the garden accent that everyone seems to crave, even in the smallest garden. Whether the feature is a small pool with a mirror-smooth surface or a great splashing cascade, water provides visual excitement and also produces pleasant sounds, which the Japanese call the music of nature. The sound of water can be almost imperceptible—a subtle dripping or rippling—or the sound can be loud, even thunderous, if the water falls from a great height onto rocks or is jetted high into the air to crash back to earth.

In Oriental landscape design, the construction of waterfalls is an art form itself. Water cascades are classified as broken or unbroken. For example, in an unbroken cascade, water may fall in an uninterrupted solid sheet, called a falling cloth, or it can fall in uninterrupted streaks, called silver threads. A fall can be broken by boulders and rock ledges that direct the flow to the left or right. Broken falls are the most naturalistic and often have several tiers requiring height.

In a small garden, such as a courtyard, a small fountain can provide a lovely water feature, producing a pleasant sound. If thought is given to design and placement, water sounds can even mask undesirable noises, such as the sound of traffic.

On the other hand, the still water of ponds and pools can produce exquisite reflections, doubling the beauty of the garden. Whether they are clear enough to see colorful fish swimming below the surface or opaque and mysterious, ponds and pools offer a wide variety of creative opportunities.

Shelters

Of all the structures in a garden, a shelter—a gazebo, summerhouse, or temple—probably introduces the strongest design statement, since it is conspicuous enough to be seen from a long distance. You can find a variety of styles in mail-order sources—Victorian, Oriental, or Italianate, for example—or you can design something distinctive of your own.

A greenhouse is the most difficult garden structure to site in a garden. Greenhouses made of plastic and fiberglass can look especially ugly, since the panes discolor with age. Although glass is certainly the preferred glazing material, even clear glass panes can look garish unless the structure is well designed. While utilitarian, freestanding aluminum-frame greenhouses are probably the most durable and are maintenance-free, they are also an eyesore. Plan to mask the greenhouse itself by planting around it, or consider attaching your greenhouse to the house as a room extension and choose a design that adds some architectural interest.

Work to combine the right accents for your garden and place them so that they and the plants are shown to the best visual and emotional advantage. The symbolic relationship between plants and structural garden accents, each enhancing the other, is an essential ingredient for excellent garden design.

An arbor of Grecian columns topped with rough-hewn beams gives this garden path a lovely romantic quality. You feel as if you were walking through ancient ruins overgrown with wild vines. When planning an arbor be sure it blends well with the rest of the garden in size and style. The pillars here are comfortably sized in relation to the large shrubs on either side. The long path and the bordering plants evoke the same blend of classic formality and natural beauty. In a smaller space, or among shorter plants, scale down proportionately.

Placed in the right position, an arbor frames a vista like a picture window. This plain arbor, decorated with climbing roses, also marks the entrance to another garden room, its height a pleasing contrast to the mostly low-growing plants beyond.

An arbor does not have to be an expensive formal addition to the garden. A simple wooden structure such as the one shown here is not hard to build. This design looks especially inviting overgrown with a drooping plant such as wisteria, because its open grid pattern allows the long flower panicles to fall enticingly into the covered space. The effect is equally dramatic on a smaller scale.

▶

The classic vine to grow over an arbor is a climbing rose. The hybrid called "American Pillar" is an outstanding choice for the job. Known as a rambling rose, it is a vigorous grower that in spring produces large clusters of carmine-pink blossoms with white centers. It's an easy rose to train and can survive in cold climates.

▼

Use arbors to create a transition from one garden space to another. Here a simple arching form covered with lath draws the focus to the gate in a charming country garden. Its height is also a flattering contrast to the ground cover garden in front. Notice the matching arbor opposite this one at the far side of the garden.

▲

Make a small garden feel bigger by placing an arbor on the property boundary to give the sense that the garden continues to the other side. This arbor also functions as an alcove, with chairs inside making a comfortable spot to read, talk, and contemplate.

◀

Consider a creative variation on espaliered fruit trees by training them over an arbor. Apple trees make this long arbor a delightful shady tunnel. In the spring, the blossoms transform it into a bower of white scented flowers, and in autumn the apples are within reach for easy picking.

Set at a distance in a strategic spot, a garden bench is both a visual focal point and a destination. Once there, it is a pleasure to sit and enjoy a view of where you've come from. Nowadays the look of classic white wrought-iron garden furniture is achieved with cast aluminum. Lighter and more rust-resistant than iron, it's a successful example of new technology improving on the beauty of old.

Situate a bench where the view is especially stunning. Even if you don't own the land you're looking at, sitting there gives a marvelous sense of being "lord of all you survey." This English teak, Chippendale-style bench is a welcome resting spot after an uphill walk, and the view over the blooming azaleas to the gardens below makes it worth the effort to get there.

Americans have always been fascinated with furniture that moves. The porch or garden swing was originally developed in the 1880s and became increasingly popular with the growth of suburbia. It is enjoying a renaissance today as more people than ever spend time in their gardens. If you want a swing, but don't have a tree or porch from which to hang it, look into the many freestanding designs.

In winter a well-designed bench works like a sculpture in a barren landscape. Snowfall accentuates the Chinese pattern in this bench shown in springtime above. Teak is an excellent wood for garden furniture because it weathers to a lovely silvery gray and can survive the elements for decades.

Claude Monet saw an unpainted version of these benches at the Petite Hameau at Versailles and was so taken with the design that he copied it. He painted his benches green to match the shutters of his house in Giverny, France (see page 174), which is a good way to create a sense of unity between house and garden. Benches in a similar style are available in North America through some garden mail-order catalogs.

Sir Edwin Lutyens, the famous English Edwardian architect who worked closely with landscape designer Gertrude Jekyll, created the flowing lines of this now-classic garden bench. Notice how the untreated teak has weathered to a beautiful silvery gray.

This classic Oriental-style bench is a thick, naturally shaped slice of tree trunk set on wooden blocks, making a striking piece in harmony with its surroundings. Use your imagination to design a bench of natural materials, creating something that is unique to you and your garden.

Different regions of the country are known for different styles of garden furniture. Choosing a style that is either native to your region or particularly unusual there adds interest to your garden. New England gardens often include an Adirondack chair. In Charleston, South Carolina, the Battery bench, named after the fortified waterfront in Charleston (now a public park), is very common. The Battery bench, shown here, has decorative wrought-iron legs and armrests, which support the wooden back and seat. The seat curves to fit the body, making it surprisingly comfortable.

◄ In addition to attracting birds, a pretty birdhouse is a charming garden feature. Houses range in style from the basic box to thatched cottages to formal designs. Here at Ladew Topiary Garden in Maryland, a large, multifamily Oriental-style birdhouse mimics the shape of the tulips below.

Attract birds to an herb garden by using a birdbath as an ornament, instead of a sundial or statue. Then give yourself a spot to sit in comfort and enjoy both the delicious scents of the garden and the antics of the birds splashing in the water. ►

This hollowed-out stone, probably once an Indian mortar for grinding acorns or grain, makes a beautiful naturalistic birdbath. Notice that the ground cover in front is very low and the azaleas behind are a dwarf variety, so the stone isn't obscured by its surroundings. ►

▲ Birdbaths come in a wide range of designs from austere to elaborate and fanciful. Choose a style that fits the atmosphere of your garden, and place it carefully, as you would a sculpture. Here a tall birdbath is a centerpiece in a round pond. Its formal, classic style complements the well-groomed garden surroundings.

▲
The iron trellis covering this Japanese-style bridge in Claude Monet's garden was an afterthought, but it was an inspired idea. Draped in blue and white wisteria, the vine-covered trellis transforms the bridge into a romantic focal point. As with the benches on page 101, the bridge and ironwork are painted green to match the shutters on Monet's house (see page 174).

▶
Choose a color for your bridge that ties it to other elements in the landscape. This gently arching bridge is a modified "moon bridge," inspired from Japanese gardens. The cheerful yellow is echoed in the yellow leaves of the trees beyond, creating a feeling of harmony in the garden. The Japanese often choose even bolder colors, such as bright red or orange, for their bridges.

▲
A little turf-covered stone bridge blends beautifully into a rural environment. To create a grass-covered bridge, simply put earth over the bridge to a depth of 6 or 8 inches (make sure the bridge is strong enough to carry the weight), and plant grass seed. You may also want to be sure your turf bridge can carry the weight of a lawn tractor.

◀

Originally designed by the Japanese, this flat, zigzag bridge made of massive planks of wood is simple to build and visually interesting. Notice that the ground cover grows right up to the edge of the bridge, and the path on the other side is moved over a few feet to accommodate it. The one flat stone, set as a welcome mat before the planks, is a clever touch, as it marks the surface change from gravel to wood.

▼

It would be an easy matter to step over a rivulet such as this one, but the bridge, comprised of a single monumental stone, is much more appealing than a gap. It provides continuity, both physically and visually.

▼

Crossing a bridge can be like a rite of passage. Use a bridge to link one part of your garden to another. Here a rustic bridge marks the transition between an open, sunny lawn and a wild, shady woodland area. In fact, a small stream divides the two spaces, but it isn't necessary for the bridge to pass over water.

▲

Bridges don't have to cross water. Many Japanese gardens contain a stream of stones that "flows" through the garden like a dry river bed. Here a simple bridge made of slabs of granite crosses a pebble "river," helping to increase the illusion of water. The charcoal gray flecks in the granite echo the dark gray stones below.

Grow winter-tender plants in containers, and move them indoors during the cold season. If you are fortunate enough to have a greenhouse or conservatory, the potted plants can over-winter there; if not, contract with a local nursery to store them. These sasanqua camellias, which have been trained as small trees, will serve as flowering houseplants during the early winter months.

Plastic containers are the most water-efficient but the least attractive. One way to solve the dilemma of what kind of pot to use is to set a practical plastic container inside a more beautiful one, such as this terra-cotta pot. The space between the pots is filled with gravel to keep the roots cooler and reduce water evaporation. In this case, the bigger pot is also better proportioned to the large crape myrtle inside it.

Cacti and succulents are especially well suited to containers because they do much better when they are root-bound. In the wild they flourish in cracks and crevices. By growing them in containers, you also have control of how much water they get. When cacti are planted in a landscape with other plants that are all watered at once by sprinklers, they can get more water than they need. Combine different plants in one pot, such as the mixture of sedums in this arrangement, or pot one cactus on its own as a sort of living sculpture. Cluster pots together for a more complex effect.

▲

Use container plants to introduce portable color in a green landscape. Here "Apple blossom" petunias ring the edge of a circular pool, adding a splash of color to the monochrome scenery and emphasizing the circular design of the pond.

▼

Bring color to eye level by setting containers on low walls or pedestals. Here a classic cement urn is planted with a verbena that hangs gently over the edges. A few vine tendrils droop farther down, creating a modified cascade look. This urn is one of a pair acting as sentinels at the entrance to the house.

▶

Soften the architectural lines of gazebos and add a splash of bright color, with flower-filled containers used as window boxes and hanging baskets. Here tall pink cosmos planted outside the gazebo have grown up above the pansies, adding another dimension to the view.

◀

Setting containers on a gravel base is ideal for drainage, because it alleviates the problem of puddles forming around each pot. Here the pots have been grouped to create a massed floral display. Bright orange, dwarf single zinnia is excellent for pots because it grows vigorously and produces a dense display of everblooming flowers. Behind it, a yellow dwarf dahlia is combined with yellow-leafed coleus. The pale yellow heads of the *Sedum spectabile* behind will turn bright rose-pink in late summer, while dwarf globe amaranth "Buddy" provides the bold magenta color. The soft blue cup-shaped flowers in the rectangular terra-cotta pot are nierembergia, a continuously flowering annual.

Containers for the garden aren't limited to plastic, cement, and terra-cotta pots manufactured expressly for that purpose. Use your imagination to find unexpected containers that uniquely express the mood of your garden. Here rustic barrel tubs blend well with the weathered wood of the deck. Planted with an abundance of impatiens, they welcome visitors with a dramatic display of color.

Choose a low, wide container when you want the height to come from the plants, not the pot. Here a tall staked tomato is mixed with low-growing flowers to make an arrangement that is both ornamental and edible.

This wheelbarrow planted with blooming fuchsias is another example of a charming, unexpected planter. The three tall fuchsias are surrounded by spreading varieties, which cover the ground and cascade over the edge. Altogether, there are nine fuchsias growing in the barrow. In a high-density situation like this, fertilize frequently to maintain vigorous growth and bloom.

Bonsai is the ancient Japanese art of dwarfing trees by cutting back the roots. A long-lived bonsai tree is a family heirloom, passed on to succeeding generations for hundreds of years. If you are fortunate enough to have a bonsai, place it where its surroundings will best show it off. Here a white pine bonsai is positioned in front of bamboo, in a spot where backlighting highlights the tree's delicate needles. Most bonsai trees are displayed outdoors during the frost-free months and moved indoors for protection during winter.

▲

Brighten the view from both inside and outside a window by putting flowering plants on a wide sill. If the window happens to be in the kitchen, include a few potted herbs.

▲

The Swiss have elevated the concept of window boxes to glorious heights. Here two balconies are lined with densely planted boxes with a cascading variety of geranium in different shades of pink and red. If your own balcony doesn't get enough sun for geraniums, plant impatiens instead.

◄

The owner of this stunning wall of flowers achieved the look by attaching wire supports to the shutters and long planters to the wall. Rig your own supports, or buy specially designed wall brackets with wire loops sized to hold pots of varying diameters.

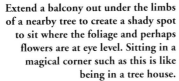

Extend a balcony out under the limbs of a nearby tree to create a shady spot to sit where the foliage and perhaps flowers are at eye level. Sitting in a magical corner such as this is like being in a tree house.

Take advantage of a beautiful view, extend living space, and provide access to the outside from rooms that are high above ground level with a raised desk. If space is available, include a two-tiered flight of stairs, which is more comfortable than a steeper single flight.

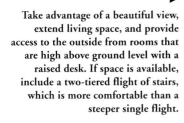

Merge your deck with the landscape by creating a peninsula, a portion of the deck that extends into the garden. The extension here, which is supported in part by a large tree stump, brings people closer to the garden than the main body of the deck; it is also a raised vantage point from which to survey the patterns, textures, and colors of foliage and flowers below.

Consider partially enclosing and covering a deck that is too sunny for sitting midday. Allow vines to grow up support posts and across overhead beams, creating a shady bower. Here a planter is also built into the structure. The profusion of potted flowers and ornamental foliage plants makes this deck a cool, refreshing retreat.

▶ The vast expanse of this large deck could be overwhelming if not for the visual interest created by the matching planters filled with soft pink impatiens that run along the sides and down the stairs. The triangular pattern created where the deck's planks change direction at one end adds to the visual interest.

▶ Rather than cut down a beautiful old tree to accommodate a deck or balcony, build around the trunk. Here the tree provides shade, as well as looking like a monumental triptych sculpture.

▲ Enhance the romance of a balcony by training a climbing rose to meet it. Here "New Dawn" is entwined around the railing, creating a sheet of blossoms that hang over the edge. This tall, upright, spreading rose will continue to produce pale pink flowers throughout the season. As the flowers age they bleach to white.

◀ Increase your living space and provide a handsome transition between indoors and out with a large, well-designed deck. This deck functions as three additional rooms. The two on the upper level are connected by a "hallway." Notice the planter built into the corner by the stairs. It brings the garden up to the level of the deck, uniting the two spaces. Shallow, wide steps lead to a lower "room" that is at the same level as the garden. The built-in seats around the lower deck double as the rim.

An espalier can be a striking feature even in winter. When the branches of this ancient apricot were young and supple, the choice ones were tied to the supporting trellis to form a fan shape. The plant was pruned to maintain the shape, as well as to create plenty of air circulation that prevents rot. Flowering branches are concentrated at the top of the wall as a decorative capping.

Espalier along a fence is known by the French name *cordon*, meaning "rope." A cordon is a good space-saving approach to espalier if you don't have a suitable wall. In fact, espaliered fruit trees often perform better in the open like this because sunny walls can get very hot.

In addition to woody trees and shrubs, trailing vines, such as ivy or creeping fig *(Ficus pumila)*, are as easy to train as espalier. Here the plant has been trained to cover a decorative trellis. Any frame, such as a trellis, provides a useful guide for pruning.

Pyracantha looks particularly dramatic when well espaliered. In the spring it's a mass of tiny white blossoms, and in the fall and winter months it's covered with clusters of red, orange, or yellow berries, depending on the variety.

A zigzag or worm fence is a rustic structure that conjures images of pioneer days. Early settlers used it because the fence is easy and quick to build without nails. Landowners simply chopped down trees and stacked the logs in a zigzag pattern to keep them standing.

When a tall fence is needed to keep out deer and you don't want the garden to feel too enclosed, build a wooden fence with spaces between each slat rather than a solid barrier. Notice the round peephole cut in the gate. It's a whimsical design feature, inspired by Japanese moon gates, which allows an unobstructed view to the space beyond.

Combine different materials to make a wall or fence more interesting; here brick posts support wooden lath. The open pattern of the fence lightens the structure, preventing it from being too imposing and also allows a limited view through to the garden, while the brick gives it a solid look.

To make a medieval-style wattle fence, simply weave supple green branches between supporting stakes. Wattle fences, built low as an edging, as shown here, or taller, are particularly effective in herb gardens.

A picket fence suits just about any style home except one that is very modern, ethnic, or elegant. Use one to enclose an old-fashioned, cottage, or Colonial garden. Here the plants have been allowed to grow through the spaces in the fence. The slats act like a frame, highlighting the brilliant color of the rhododendron flowers.

Solve the problem of enclosing sloping land or land that changes levels dramatically by "stair-stepping" the fence. Brick walls can be stepped in the same way.

Grow a flowering, trailing plant up and over the top to make a drab fence seem to come alive with color. Shown here are ivy-leaf geraniums (Pelargonium peltatum). Bougainvillea, which grows in warm regions, is another low-maintenance plant that will cover a fence or wall with a riot of color.

Choose a fountain that fits the style of your house and garden. Here elements of Spanish and Japanese design are combined by designer Cevan Forristt to create a uniquely Californian amalgam of the two cultures. The Japanese bamboo serves as water pipes, while the adobe wall and base reflect a southwestern style.

Choose an unexpected place for a fountain, such as the middle of this man-made pond. A miniaturized version of the giant water spout that shoots up out of Lake Geneva, this fountain produces lively sound and movement in a wooded area.

Add humor and whimsy to your garden design with a fountain such as this spouting snail, which appears to streak along the surface of the pool. This fountain is a unique variation on the spouting animal motif.

You don't need a lot of room to fit in a fountain and pond. Here a face sculpture designed by Los Angeles artist Dick Rosmini takes so little space it is ideal in a confined city garden. Water gurgling softly through the mouth adds a dimension of sound to the garden, and the low pond serves as a focal point.

A garden with multiple "rooms" is exciting and satisfying. Define a garden room with walls or hedges, or simply by changing levels and/or styles. Here the beds intersected by a path on the upper level form one room. The broad flagstone terrace beyond is another room with a different look and function. In a very small garden, you can make rooms simply by broadening a path to create a small seating space.

Carve a small terrace out of a hillside to create a private garden room. The trees and ground covers bordering this patch of lawn enclose and define the space.

Enclose a garden space, leaving only one opening, by encircling it with a dense hedge. This secret spot is paved with flagstone. If you prefer, leave the area unpaved for planting. A place like this should be a soul-satisfying retreat.

You don't need a lot of land to create a garden room. Create a protected seating area in any corner, as in this city garden. A row of bricks facing one direction marks the transition from the path to the patio, and flowering trees and shrubs give the feeling that the walls of the garden room have been covered with a pretty floral wallpaper.

▼

Choose a gate in keeping with local style and history. This elegant gate borders the Governor's Palace property in Colonial Williamsburg and provides access to the British soldiers' graveyard. To maintain the historical look of the area, the owner had the gate custom-made and enhanced the design by adding a slated fence section on either end.

►

To alleviate the imposing, solid form of a wall, choose an open-style gate such as this one made of spindles that allows a glimpse into the wonders of the garden. A solid gate would have been more private, but less open and welcoming.

◄

On a large estate it is convenient and attractive to install a double gate for vehicles and a single one for pedestrians. Made of vertical metal bars, these gates allow a view down the driveway, but are secure when shut and locked. Notice that the single gate to the side is a matching, scaled-down version of the large double gate.

This gate design is a modified version of a Japanese moon gate, westernized to blend with the white lattice fence. In keeping with the Western taste for symmetry, two matching gates have been built to face each other. The resulting view through one "moon" to the other provides a fresh perspective on the garden and invites entry.

The maxim "less is more" sometimes applies to gates. It's not always appropriate for them to stand out as a design feature. In this historical Colonial vegetable garden, the gate is the natural continuation of a simple, moss-covered fence.

A gate latch, like accessories to an outfit, is the finishing touch that can make or break the look. Choose one as carefully as you choose the gate itself. This Quaker-style sliding latch was handmade, in keeping with the texture of the gate and the tone of the American Colonial garden.

You don't have to pair a white picket fence with a traditional vertical slatted gate. Make your property unique by choosing a gate that varies in design and color. Notice how the square within a square pattern forms a sort of bull's eye centered on the house in the background.

A gazebo is both an architectural feature in a garden and a sheltered spot to sit and admire a view. Depending on the situation, you may want it to stand out as a dramatic focal point or blend with its surroundings. Set in the woods, this gazebo merges with its environment in an aesthetically pleasing way. The round, upright posts echo the tree trunks, while the low lattice walls maintain the open feeling of the structure.

If you want to evoke a specific period in history or an ethnic landscape style in your garden, a structure will do it more quickly than plants. Here an old-fashioned gazebo recalls the elegant days of the Victorian era, providing both a visual and an intellectual focus in the garden.

A topographic challenge such as this sloping site can be turned to advantage with a clever plan and may be the ideal place for a gazebo. Here a large gazebo was incorporated into the design of the deck and built of the same materials. It looks out to a panoramic view across rolling lawns. On two sides, the gazebo wall does double duty by retaining the sloping earth and serving as a planter for multicolored impatiens, which become a bright color accent against the weathered wood and stone.

◄

You may wish to locate a gazebo to mark the transition from one part of a garden to another, as well as to provide a spot to sit. Here a small gazebo with Greek temple–like columns serves as the portal to an enchanted garden enclave, enhancing its spiritual quality.

◄

Place a gazebo at the top of a hill or at another vantage point where it becomes a protected area to rest and enjoy the surroundings. This quaint gazebo was built of local stone, so while it is a monumental structure, it is in harmony with the area.

►

The edge of a pool or pond is an excellent place to build a gazebo, where it reflects beautifully on the water. The cut-out hearts and flowers along the sides of this gazebo, the deeply pitched conical roof, and the two-story birdhouse on top make it all the more interesting visually, both directly and in reflection.

A traditional Victorian gazebo goes especially well with a romantic flower garden. Since a gazebo is not hard to build, many mail-order companies now offer gazebo kits in a wide choice of sizes and styles.

A gazebo can be anything from a very rustic shelter to an elegant, ornate structure. On the formal extreme is this cupola-topped gazebo that graces the famous Bagatelle rose garden in the Bois de Boulogne in Paris.

Use a three-sided gazebo in a spot where the view is not worthy of a 360-degree vantage, such as at the end of an enclosed property or the beginning of a dense wood. Notice here how an arching trellis frames the gazebo and the flower-lined path draws the eye to its center, both giving the structure a heightened sense of importance.

If biting insects are a problem, screen in your gazebo to create an outdoor haven from pests. This elaborately furnished lakeside screened room even features a wood-burning stove for chilly evenings. If you plan to spend a lot of time sitting in your gazebo, don't hesitate to equip it with amenities.

▶

Combine hanging baskets and potted plants to decorate a covered porch. Notice that the petunias and marigolds growing in the bed in front of the porch railing are the same as those in the pots above, adding color and unity to the scene.

▼

Break up the monotony of a large blank wall with a basket filled with profusely flowering plants hanging from a wall bracket. Here cascading pink lobelia and nasturtiums are mixed with upright geraniums and dusty miller to create a happy medley of color and bloom.

◀

Decorate a covered porch or balcony with flowering pots hung between the supporting pillars. The nasturtiums shown here grow particularly well with less sun. Turn the pots regularly so all sides of the plants are exposed to the light; otherwise, the growth and bloom may become lopsided.

◀

Hang a multitude of pots or baskets full of blooming plants from a lath cover to create a pleasant retreat from the sun. The filtered shade created by the lath is the ideal environment for plants such as these tuberous begonias and fuchsias. A lath house is also a good place to revive tired houseplants.

◄ Train and prune two hedges flanking a path to create a spectacular living arch. In this garden the spreading deciduous hornbeam *(Carpinus)* was chosen so that in the fall the gateway would be a blaze of color. Notice that an arched trellis beneath the hedge serves as both a frame and pruning

◄ You don't need to be a slave to pruning to have a hedge. Many shrubs, such as this slow-growing boxwood, can be left to grow naturally, producing a pleasing billowing effect.

Fast-growing eugenia is an excellent shrub when you want a hedge quickly. A young plant will grow to 6 or 8 feet in just a few years. Eugenia is frost-sensitive, however, so it is suitable only in mild climates. ►

A hedge should always be pruned slightly wider at the bottom than at the top so that light and air can reach more of the surface of the plant. An extreme example, this Canada hemlock *(Tsuga canadensis)* has been pruned to a shape that is more cone-like than boxed. ►

◄ Create a sweet-scented blooming hedge of lilac *(Syringa)* by planting the shrubs close together. The exact distance will depend on the growth patterns of the variety you choose. In frost-free climates, make a flowering hedge of camellia instead.

◄ Create a checkerboard effect by planting a row of azaleas, or another shrub, in two alternating, high-contrast flower or leaf colors. Here the plants have been left unpruned. A more tailored version of this can be achieved by sheering the plants into a box shape each year after their bloom.

For a low-growing flowering hedge in mild climates, plant the gray-leaved euryops *(Euryops pectinatus)*. It's an upright, evergreen shrub that produces a profusion of bright yellow daisylike flowers in early spring and continues to bloom sporadically the rest of the year. ►

Euonymus alata, which is available in evergreen and deciduous varieties, makes an excellent shrub or hedge. It comes in a wide choice of leaf color combinations ranging from dark green to bright yellow, as well as variegated silver and gold. The dark green leaves of deciduous euonymus turn flaming red during the autumn months, earning it the nickname "burning bush." ►

◄ Pyracantha, a versatile plant, can be espaliered (see page 111), grown as a single shrub, or trained as a hedge. It is covered in orange-red berries in the fall, and small, creamy white flowers all spring. There are varieties suitable for every region.

◄ The clusters of star-shaped pink flowers that cover Indian hawthorn *(Raphiolepis indica)* during spring and early summer make it an attractive hedge for mild-climate regions. An added bonus: it is a tidy, low-maintenance plant that is drought- and heat-tolerant.

▼
Cut a straight edge, with a flat-blade garden spade to create a clean break at the edge of a lawn. Here the edge marks the transition between the flat grass and the lemon thyme *(Thymus Serpyllum)* that covers the slope.

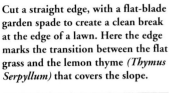

▲
In contrast to grasses such as zoysia and other clump-forming varieties that turn brown in cold weather, improved perennial rye grass will remain green in all but the coldest winters.

Choose your varieties of grass carefully to suit your specific setting. The best drought-tolerant grasses are Bermuda, St. Augustine, and zoysia. Fescue is most successful for shady lawns; it also tolerates salty soil. In areas that get high traffic or heavy wear from children playing, plant hardy varieties such as perennial rye or zoysia. For a perfect-looking lawn that meets the rigorous standards of Wimbledon, choose bentgrass, a fine-blade grass, but be aware that you must water and feed it regularly.

▲
Consider a free-form shape rather than an unimaginative rectangle of lawn edged with shrubs. Here the lawn wraps around the corners of the house in a pleasing serpentine line. In addition to bordering shrubs, brightly colored flowers add a dynamic element to the design.

◄
In deeply shaded areas, where moss is already growing, consider encouraging it and letting it spread to create a moss lawn, rather than trying to get grass to grow. Take a soil test, and add sulphur, if necessary, to increase the acidity. Divide and plug the existing moss to help it spread, or collect more from local woods. It replenishes itself easily so you are not robbing the environment.

▼
To create an element of mystery and surprise in a garden, allow paths to curve so that what's beyond is out of sight. Here slabs of stone serve as steps to cope with the sudden change in level, then the gravel path winds behind a hedge, enticing pedestrians to follow it.

▼
Even in a tiny garden, a path gives a sense of somewhere to go. Just provide a reason for using it, such as a bench where you can relax and enjoy the garden. Here a cement bench has been set on the perimeter of the garden, making it feel larger than it is. The primrose-lined stepping stone path leading to the bench also provides an opportunity to walk among flowers.

◄
Brick paths can create a variety of moods, depending on the way they are laid out. Here, brick laid in a "running bond" design follows the curve of a path, creating a design that evokes currents flowing in a river. For a tailored look, consider a straight or diagonal herringbone design. Other classic brick-laying patterns include a fan motif and "basket weave," a staggered design.

◄
The Japanese are particularly good at designing gardens that are enhanced by the weather. A path of gray, rounded river stones takes on a glossy sheen when it's wet. Notice that the paving surface changes to gravel beyond the wooden frame. Even with your eyes closed you know that you've passed into another garden room because the two materials feel and sound different beneath your feet.

Create a grand allée or avenue by planting trees equidistant in parallel lines along a path or drive. Here the branches of American beech trees *(Fagus grandifolia)* were carefully interlaced when they were young and supple in a process called pleaching, but the look is equally effective when the trees are allowed to grow untrained.

Plant a walkway with grass to give a sense of continuity between lawns and adjoining paths. Grass is soft on the feet and soothing to the eyes.

Use local stone to give a path an indigenous look. This cobbled walkway has a natural, informal feeling well suited to a cottage-style garden of annual and perennial flowers. Because the stones were set in the ground without cement, the plants are free to spread into the path, where the occasional "volunteer" may take root in the middle. Weeds in the path are kept to a minimum by limiting irrigation in this otherwise dry California garden.

▶

Terra-cotta tile is an excellent patio surface, particularly if the house is in a Mediterranean design. It is easy to clean, and its warm rusty color is restful on the eyes in bright sun. Here the low stone and cement wall along one side gives the patio a pleasant enclosed feeling without blocking the view. Across each end, the vista is framed by "picture windows" created by wisteria-covered trellises.

▶

Allow a path to spread at one point to create an intimate, space-saving patio deep in the garden. In this suburban lot, an illusion of greater size is created by paths that twist and turn throughout the space, sometimes coming very close to each other, but separated visually by dense foliage. This patio is one of several clearings in the jungle.

▲

Transform an odd corner of the garden into a special patio enclave. Inexpensive gravel paving keeps the spot from getting muddy, as well as setting a rustic tone enhanced by the weathered chairs. A tree stump supports the sliced wood tabletop; another stump behind holds a potted succulent. The screen of dense passionflower vine *(Passiflora)* makes the place feel set apart from the rest of the garden.

◀

An ideal place for a patio is beside a pool or pond, especially when the design works as well as this one by landscape architects Wolfgang Oehme and James van Sweden. The edge of the patio juts over the rectangular pool, creating the illusion that the flagstone is floating on the water. When wet, the flagstone has a watery sheen of its own. The table repeats both the shape and materials of the patio, adding unity to the scene.

▲ It is best to make a pool, even though man-made, look at ease in its surroundings. Uneven stones edging the random shape of this woodland pool make the edges look natural, while plants spilling over the sides soften the hardness of the stone. The statue of a cherub sitting on the edge helps create the sense that you've stumbled upon a magic moment in the woods—which indeed you have.

Build a lily pond in a sheltered corner of your garden. Here an edging of stone is an attractive, natural transition between the grass and the water. Pots of shade-loving begonias, impatiens, and ferns sit on the back edge and on the wall behind the pond, drawing the eye to this pretty spot in the lawn. ▶

▲ Transform a blank wall into a vision of beauty by building a pool and fountain into it. Pots of blooming plants placed on the edges of this raised pool and others wired to the wall break up the expanse of brick (see page 108). The low, clipped hedge echoes the boxy edge of the pool.

Enjoy the serenity of watching gold-fish, as shown here, or the more exotic (and expensive) Japanese koi (which means "brocaded carp"), swim in a garden pool. This pool has a distinct Japanese style with the arched bridge, monumental stones jutting into the water, stone lantern, and edging of logs standing on end.

Ferns and hostas, with their diverse leaf forms and colors, are excellent plants to grow around shady ponds. They both soften the edges and help give the setting a naturalistic feeling.

This formal scalloped bowl and foun-tain set on a pedestal in an octagonal pool add height and a focal point to a flat terrace of mosaic pebbles. Notice that the bottom of the pool is paved with the same stones as the terrace, except they have been laid flat rather than on edge. Put pots of bright flow-ering plants around a pool such as this to add a colorful living element to the design.

Enhance a patio with a miniature water garden. Here a small, round pool functions as a large planter for the water lilies that cover the surface. The ivy embracing the side of the pond joins softscape and hardscape in a pleasing union.

These two ponies, almost buried in the lavish foliage, lend a sense of fantasy to this woodland setting. Locate sculpture in the garden where it will surprise, charm, and please the eye.

▼

A statue provides a focal point in a garden. Here a whippet sitting next to an urn accentuates a bend in the path and marks the point where the path branches in two directions.

The owner of this property commissioned sculptor Charles Parks to immortalize her two young daughters in bronze. The statues are on pedestals in the round pond, adding a special, very personal touch to the garden. Whether or not you can afford similar images of your own children, consider placing a statue in or near a pool or pond (see page 127).

This carved wooden pelican, encrusted with bārnacles and shells from the sea, looks completely at home on what looks like a pier piling next to the wooden deck. Don't be satisfied until you find a sculpture that fits your setting. This small town garden is just a block from the Pacific Ocean, where pelicans are a natural part of the environment.

Elevate a small sculpture to eye level by placing it on a pedestal. Here the gray marble of this classical bust is set off by a background formed by the broad, dark green leaves of a climbing rose.

Add a touch of humor to your garden with a small sculpture such as this stalking cat placed on the low wall where it can be seen. The gracefully arching ivy leaves make an attractive frame and backdrop to the sculpture, and keep it from being intrusive.

A modern garden calls for a modern sculpture. Here a reclining woman basks in the sun while she views amber stalks of ornamental grass.

Homeowners who aspire to topiary, but haven't the time or patience to train and prune a slow-growing shrub, can obtain a similar effect very quickly by growing a vine over a small wire frame. Here four yew plants are being grown up the legs and through the body of a goat; English ivy will cover the frame just as effectively in less time.

This statue doubles as a sundial and is an amusing pun for those alert enough to notice that the little boy is sitting in a bed of thyme.

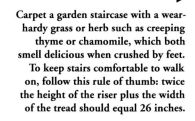

Carpet a garden staircase with a wear-hardy grass or herb such as creeping thyme or chamomile, which both smell delicious when crushed by feet. To keep stairs comfortable to walk on, follow this rule of thumb: twice the height of the riser plus the width of the tread should equal 26 inches.

The cobweb sedum growing out of the risers of this staircase helps retain the soil and is an intriguing decorative element. The treads are made of flagstone cemented into place.

▲
Overlapping round millstones, available from well-stocked garden supply stores, stack easily to create stairs where there is an abrupt level change on a narrow, informal path. This design is a study in rounded shapes with the globular boulders edging the stairs, the flowing curve of the path, and the millstones themselves.

When designing a staircase, choose a style and material that are in keeping with your surroundings. Stone slabs are the perfect material for stairs in this rocky hillside. Besides blending with the environment, the horizontal stones forming the stairs echo the angular, vertical upthrustings of the wall of stone to the left.

Save space by building a dramatic spiral staircase to lead from one level to another. This staircase is made of wood to unite it with the wooden balcony above. Notice that the supporting beams for the stairs match those of the balcony. The pots of blooming geraniums evenly spaced down the outer edge of the stairs emphasize the beautiful flowing lines and add a touch of color.

▲

Brightly painted tiles set in the risers of a stairway add a Spanish look to a garden. Use the painted tiles in conjunction with adobe or stucco walls and terra-cotta tiles as shown here, or with other materials, to give just a hint of a Mediterannean style.

◄

Wood is an excellent inexpensive material for garden stairs. Be sure to use a type that can withstand weather. On the West Coast, redwood is the preferred choice. Southern gardens usually feature cypress, and pressure-treated pine is used in the Northeast. Here naturally weathered wood stairs complement picket fencing atop the stone wall and bounding the property, enhancing the sense of unity and belonging.

Line a stream with stones to give it a border and to protect the bank from washing away. In this case, the outlining stones emphasize the attractive curve of the brook. This classical Japanese footbridge is strong enough to support the weight of a tractor, making mowing on both sides a simple matter.

▲

When you buy a piece of property with a stream on it, chances are the edges will be an overgrown wasteland. For an easy, immediate treatment, clear out the side nearest the house and plant lawn to the edge. Allow the opposite side to remain as is, making the stream the transition between cultivated and wild areas. Notice how the stones placed in this stream create interesting currents.

▲

If you have both a stream and a sloping property, use your imagination to devise interesting ways to run water downhill. Here a man-made rill, interrupted by occasional small falls, runs straight and narrow down the slope. Another possibility is to design a series of streams, each making a different sound.

◄

A stepping stone path runs the length of this rivulet to create an unusual passage through the meadow and shrubs. Boulders and stones, whether set in a tight row as shown here or spaced randomly in a larger stream, are an attractive addition to flowing water.

▲

A swimming pool doesn't have to be a jarring interruption in the landscape. This pool fits in easily with the sloping rock garden. Flat paving stones that blend with the boulders on the hill edge the pool; at the rock garden end, the plants grow right up to the edge. An occasional stone set on end in the patio works like a modern sculpture in the landscape.

▶

Tie your garden design to the surrounding landscape by echoing elements. This free-form pool looks like a miniature version of the estuary beyond. The large gray boulders near the Jacuzzi are repeated in miniature in the stone wall and the partition between the pool and spa. The gray is also picked up by the flagstone decking. As a result, the near and distant scenes create a peaceful, unified whole.

▲

Tie the pool to the design of your home by echoing an architectural feature from the house. Here the shape of the pool repeats the angular lines of the dormer windows. The pleasing result is an interesting-looking pool with a zigzag edge that allows room for a spacious bricked seating area.

◄ Use wide steps with a shallow rise to create miniature terraced planting beds. These terraced steps on a Pennsylvania farm were inspired by similar ones in the garden at Great Dixter, which belongs to the well-known English garden writer Christopher Lloyd. Planted with alpine plants and dwarf bulbs, they make an unusual rock garden.

◄ Build a narrow terrace, such as this raised stone planter, to create a transition between a porch and garden. The planter brings the flowers up to a level where they can be seen from the porch; this is more attractive than leaving the blank porch wall exposed to the path.

▲ Terracing is a time-honored method for reclaiming steep slopes into useful planting space. The material you choose for retaining walls should complement the style and formality of your garden. Here a stone wall, intersected with steps, retains the deeply cut soil.

► Allow plants to trail over the edge of retaining walls or terraces to create a living fringe or curtain. Here juniper "Blue Rug" (*Juniperus horizontalis*) softens the hard edge of the wall, and the different shades of green on the upper and lower levels combine to form a subtle tapestry of color.

◄

If you want to separate two spaces, but don't want a solid barrier, use a trellis. The lacy design gives a glimpse into the space beyond and is a good support for climbing vines.

▼

This roofless trellised room was built as a waiting area for people who want to see the garden. In the summer, vines climbing up the sides create their own patterns on the fretwork; in winter, the structure's design and the naturally weathered wood are emphasized by the snow.

◄

A trellis can be a way to transform an uninteresting bare wall into a fascinating one. Here at Nemours, one of the Du Pont properties in Delaware, an elaborate trellis design incorporating the windows of the building gives the illusion of a formal conservatory adjoining the garden, rather than the back side of a house.

▲

The wall looming over this tiny garden would be oppressive, if not for the illusion of perspective created by the trellis. The trellis distracts attention from the expanse of wall and looks like a doorway leading to another part of the garden. The feathery trees flanking the arch also help hide the wall and create a protected spot to sit.

▶

Save on heating costs by building your greenhouse as an extension of your house. The warmth from your house is shared with the greenhouse and, on sunny days, the heat from the greenhouse radiates into your home. Greenhouses are invaluable for protecting cold-tender plants in winter and for getting a head start on spring by propagating seeds indoors.

▼

Build a box to hide your trash cans from view, in an easily accessible place. A simple partition to screen off these unsightly but necessary items can also work well. You may be surprised how much prettier your garden will look.

▲

Use a blank wall of a toolshed as one side of a cold frame. The corrugated plastic roof on this shed is an inexpensive cover and doubles as a giant skylight, admitting daylight into the building.

◀

The simple but upscale design of this toolshed, with its cedar siding and shingle roof, is a beautiful example of a service building fitting into and even enhancing the landscape. The bed of lupines in front makes the shed seem more like a guest house than a storage room.

▶

Accent a view by framing it. Here an overhanging, vine-covered trellis is like a picture window overlooking the scene. A pair of elegantly coiffed sphinxes frame the vista from their perches on the edge of the terrace, while the two pool houses in the background continue the pattern of symmetrical framing.

▼

Create the illusion of a distant view with various techniques known as trompe l'oeil, from the French meaning "to deceive the eye." Here the angles of the lath create a sense of perspective, making it appear that the trellis frames a passage leading to a fountain and trees beyond. The scene is, in fact, painted on the wall.

▶

Combine elements in the landscape to draw the eye to a distant view. Here the vista begins with a brick path. The bricks lay parallel, pointing toward the stone stairs that lead up the slope to a grass path. Just beyond, almost around the corner, is the distant goal: a clearing among the tall trees. The design is visually compelling, with each element beckoning you to follow the trail to the end.

▲

Use color to define and accentuate a vista. Here at Keukenhoff gardens in the Netherlands, the bright yellow patches of daffodils in the distance are in sharp contrast to the deep blue river of *Muscari armeniacum*, drawing the eye to the end. Use the same principles on a smaller scale by putting a bright flower accent at the back of a scene with a deeper color in front.

▲

Dress up a wall with ornaments such as this spouting lion's head fountain. Other possibilities include painted tiles, a sculpture that doesn't spout water, decorative outdoor clocks, outdoor thermometers, and hanging baskets (see page 121).

▼

Transform a bare wall into a living feature in your garden by covering it with a vine. Here the creeping fig *(Ficus pumila)* hugs the wall so closely you can still see the recessed design. This tender vine needs no pruning to keep it looking manicured, and it will grow in a very narrow strip of exposed earth.

▶

Add interest to a wall and create a division between two spaces by grooming a hedge to look like a medieval flying buttress. Since a hedge generally adds a strong architectural element to a design, this treatment is a visual double entendre. This garden feature is particularly appropriate in a traditional garden or an older property.

▲

Place a wide balustrade against a wall and use it as a decorative shelf for pots. Dwarf lemons, which are an attractive color accent against this brick expanse, do particularly well here because they get extra warmth from the heat radiating off the wall.

An old dry stone wall is often host to a number of plants, including lichen, moss, and tenacious shallow-rooted flowers. When building a dry wall, pack soil between the stones so plants can root more easily.

Dry stone walls are built without benefit of bonding cement. These sturdy walls blend beautifully into the landscape when they are made of local material. It's a fine art to stack the stones so the wall will be structurally sound, but worth the trouble. The hillsides of England's Lake District and Yorkshire Dales are crisscrossed with dry stone walls, a strikingly beautiful hallmark of those regions.

Allow a low-spreading plant, such as this creeping spruce (*Picea abies* "Reflexa"), to spill over the side of a wall to create a cascading waterfall effect. Here the exposed parts of the wall are growing with lichen, adding additional texture and color.

▲ Take advantage of a sloping property by building a series of waterfalls spilling into lily pools. Here the water is recirculated so that it bubbles up into the pool at the top level before starting its return journey downward.

A slender stream of falling water, known as a "silver thread" in Oriental landscape design, is a very delicate form of waterfall. Here the water trickles into a tiny pool, creating a glittering spray as it hits a stone. ▶

▲ The sound of falling water is the music of nature. You can orchestrate the sound by guiding the water so that it ripples over pebbles, crashes from a great height, or moves slowly around obstacles in its path such as rocks and logs. You also have control of the pattern of flow. Here a boulder splits the stream, so there are two ribbons falling from the second drop.

Shooting water out of a spout over-head creates this "rainbow falls." As it sprays out, the droplets hit boulders and rocks that have been carefully arranged below. The drops splinter again to form a fine mist that refracts the sun, causing a rainbow. Although this is a complicated design concept, it can be done on a small scale.

A frozen waterfall, which captures a moment in time until the thaw, is like an ice sculpture in the garden. Broad, evergreen rhododendron leaves are a pleasing contrast at the edge of the shining ice.

Run a large volume of water over a ledge so that it spreads out like a curtain to create a "falling cloth" water-fall. If possible, create a ledge that juts out far enough so there is room for a path behind the fall. It is a magical experience to walk behind a sheet of water and look back at the world through a watery screen while keeping relatively dry.

Garden Habitats

DEALING WITH A difficult landscape habitat offers the joy and challenge of transforming a problem—such as a swampy ground or deep shade—into an asset. This chapter presents ideas for handling a number of environments, which may exist throughout your property or may be present in only one small part of your garden. Occasionally tricks can be employed to improve the habitat itself. Most of the time, a difficult habitat can be completely changed only at enormous cost. The wisest course is to work *with* the site, using plants that tolerate the unusual conditions and installing structures that blend with the natural setting.

The four most difficult sites are undoubtedly boggy soil, desert conditions, hillsides, and shade.

Bog

There are several conditions that produce poor drainage and boggy ground. The cause is generally either heavy clay soil or an impervious rocky subsurface that traps moisture above it. It is frequently possible to dig a trench and set drainage pipes 2 feet below the soil surface to direct excess water to a drain. Good topsoil can then be added for planting. If the waterlogged area is not too extensive, you can simply lay down a bed of crushed stone and on top of that build a raised bed of topsoil held in place by landscape ties, rocks, or bricks.

The best solution to the problem of boggy ground may be to transform it into a romantic water feature by digging a pond in the middle of the swampy area, with a stream feeding the pond if possible, and putting in families of fish to control the mosquito larvae common in wet environments. Backhoe the soil

to create a lip of high ground surrounding the water, and plant a combination of aquatic and moisture-loving plants there.

Desert

Even a desert lot, where every vestige of native plant life has been removed by a developer's bulldozer, can be improved and made to bloom again. Choose flowering cacti (such as barrel cacti) and flowering succulents (such as ice plants) that are well adapted to a harsh, dry environment. Visiting desert botanical gardens—such as those in Tucson, Phoenix, and Superior, Arizona—will stimulate a wealth of ideas and provide a source for plants that may be difficult to obtain through a regular garden center.

Also keep in mind that many desert soils are stony. Small stones, like gravel, offer a decent growing medium, since plants can grow through the stones to a considerable depth. But stony soil, like sand, is poor at retaining moisture and nutrients. Regular watering and feeding (especially with slow-release fertilizer) will yield spectacular results.

In a desert region, where water is scarce and frequently rationed, consider creating a catchment that channels precious rainfall into a reservoir. The roof of a house makes a good catchment, with gutters and downspouts directing water into a cistern. Use the water collected to water plants during dry spells.

Hillsides

A rich assortment of plants can grow on sunny slopes if erosion from rain is controlled, and if the slope can be irrigated and watered regularly.

Gradual slopes are the easiest to manage, since zigzag paths and steps can be used to gain access. Although soil on exposed slopes tends to be stony or hard clay, improved soil can be hauled to gentle slopes and anchored down with bird netting until plants have established a network of roots to prevent erosion.

Steep slopes are more difficult. You may be able to dig special planting pockets, or possibly use boulders to create planting pockets, avoiding places where water drains naturally down the slope. Or the site may require the construction of terraces made from costly stone or less expensive wooden landscape ties. With a steep slope, the easiest solution is probably a mass planting of one particular plant. In coastal areas of California, Hottentot fig—a flowering succulent from South Africa—is popular for mass planting where soil is sandy, while seaside morning glory (*Convolvulus mauritanicus),* which has beautiful flowers and heart-shaped leaves, is a more colorful option. Where irrigation is possible, vining ivy-leaf geraniums, lantana, and bougainvillea offer good alternatives.

A windy hillside may require protection before plants can take hold. Hedges make the best windbreaks because they cushion the force of the wind, unlike a solid barrier, which winds can hit and jump over, sometimes with destructive force. To establish a hedge in a windy site, however, you may need to erect a temporary barrier of burlap stapled to posts or a wall of hay bales on the windward side of the plants. Once the hedge is firmly rooted, the temporary windbreak can be removed.

Shade

Light is such a critical factor in the growth of plants that even a 1 percent improvement in light can produce a 100 percent improvement in flowering performance. Although there are many flowering plants that tolerate shade, there are many types of shade, and even a famous shade-loving plant, such as impatiens, will grow spindly and flower only sparsely in deep shade.

Constant light shade—or even deep shade for only a portion of the day—is not such a difficult condition for plants. Deep shade beneath a dense tree canopy or high walls constitutes the worst shade condition. Shade from a dense tree canopy is easily remedied by removing a few trees to admit more light or, better yet, by selectively removing a few branches. Removing even a single branch can make enough difference in light intensity to encourage a colorful flower garden. High walls, the biggest problem in most city gardens, are not so easily removed. But you can paint the base of the wall and use white limestone chips as a mulch to increase the amount of light. Shiny metal introduced in the form of a fake mirror can also reflect light into a shaded walkway.

Microclimates

You might consider creating microclimates or taking advantage of existing microclimates to extend your planting possibilities. A wisteria-covered arbor over a flagstone terrace can produce a cool canopy under which moss and ferns may grow, while a

short distance away, on a cleared, sunny slope you can have a circular sunbathing surface of white beach pebbles surrounded by a xeriscape (drought-tolerant garden) of cacti and succulents.

Every garden invariably contains microclimates. The north side of a wall is always cooler than the south side; soil under trees holds moisture longer than soil in full sun; soil blanketed with leaves or pine needles remains cooler than exposed soil; and water often has a cooling influence, especially when it is moving and shaded by trees. Even in a cold climate, look for sun traps—places where the frost and snow melts first—and consider these spots for marginally tender plants, especially if the sun trap is sheltered. Though southern magnolias and camellias are associated with warm climates, they can be grown in northern states in sheltered places.

Some of the most interesting examples of microclimates and habitat gardens are in the Huntington Botanical Gardens, north of Los Angeles. Within a short walk of an exposed, hot, dry desert garden crowded with cacti and succulents is a Japanese garden positioned in a cool, moist, sheltered valley, which is verdant with ferns and moss and has a stream running through it. In another area, a collection of drought-tolerant Australian and South African plants grow beside an aquatic garden featuring a series of waterlily ponds surrounded by sedge grass, bamboo, and papyrus.

Working with the special challenges posed by each habitat in your garden is an excellent way to achieve rich variety in your home landscape and a high level of satisfaction for you and your guests.

Mass-plant a swampy area with a damp-tolerant plant, such as this perennial *Primula japonica*. Rosettes of leaves first appear in early spring, then clusters of flowers in shades of pink and white open shortly after and last for about 2 weeks. When the flowers die, the plants create a green ground cover that looks attractive through the summer and autumn months, until the plants are killed back by frost.

Add soil to raise the banks of a low-lying pool, then densely plant with varieties that do well near water. In the summer, this northeastern pond is a colorful spot full of blooming pink *Sedum spectabile*, hostas, astilbe, and bright yellow *Rudbeckia fulgida*.

Transform a problem swampy area into an asset by choosing plants that thrive in boggy soil. These clumps of *Ligularia dentata*, with their heart-shaped leaves on long, mahogany brown stems, thrive in damp locations. They are fully hardy from zones 4 to 8 and produce orange daisylike flowers in summer. Other plants sharing this wet spot are a marsh azalea that has just finished blooming and blue forget-me-nots.

Build a boardwalk to provide a dry walkway through wet ground. This one extends through marshland and functions as a long nature trail, but the concept can be adapted to any size and is an excellent way of gaining dry access to a wet area.

In a small city lot, use perspective to give a sense of more space than is actually there. Here a pool surrounded by rounded boxwood and a little cherub at the end draw the eye down the garden, making it feel longer. The pond is scaled down to enhance the perception of distance. The simple, symmetrical design of the garden also increases the sense of size.

▼

Transform a rooftop or balcony into a jungle with a profusion of potted plants. The owner of this Philadelphia rooftop garden brings many of his cold-tender plants inside for winter. He takes cuttings from those that grow too big to move and nurtures them indoors until spring. Some nurseries will contract to store large potted specimen plants over winter if you don't have space for them.

▲

Design features serve multiple functions to save space in a small garden. Here an undulating retaining wall doubles as a seat. A bench, which follows the same curve, sits on the wall as a decorative accent. Notice that the soil in the planter has been banked, allowing more planting space and raising the flowers for a better view.

◄

Create separate spaces for different needs to make a small garden more livable. Here a small, paved seating area is more private screened by a bed of tall flowers. There is still space for a lawn, which doubles as the path to the patio. Because this garden has room for a patio, a lawn, and a flower bed, the space feels larger than it is.

▲
Ameliorate any claustrophobic feeling by planting narrow, enclosed spaces with shade-tolerant plants that are not intrusive in their spread or that accept pruning, such as the camellias shown here. Edges of the path are softened with low-growing plants on both sides, and the little cherub set among the ferns is a charming focal point at the end of this narrow walkway.

▲
In a garden with little space, grow plants vertically rather than horizontally. Layer the heights to give a sense of depth. A vine covers the two-level wall in this Charleston, South Carolina, garden. The camellias in the planter in front of the wall are underplanted with dwarf azaleas. The potted plants give an added sense of depth and interest.

▲
It's not necessary to have a large garden to indulge your sense of humor and your urge to collect unusual plants. Grow a potted conversation piece such as this calico flower (*Aristolochia gigantea*), which blooms in summer. Although tender below 55° F, it is a fast-growing vining evergreen that can be propagated from cuttings each autumn so new plants will be ready by spring.

▲
Mask city noise and add charm to a neglected corner of the garden with a small fountain. This one, designed by Cevan Forristt, harmonizes beautifully with the wall of the house, so it is noticed for its original, creative design and does not feel obtrusive in the small space (see page 114).

Grow cacti in pots to enjoy their diverse and unusual plant forms. Echinopsis hybrids, called Easter lily cacti or sea urchin cacti, are loved for their dramatic flower that comes in many bright colors. Keep cacti out-doors during warm weather or in a sunny window when the air is cool. Be careful not to overwater. Small cacti thrive with only 1 tablespoon of water per plant per month. To encourage abundant blooms, increase watering during early spring to simu-late desert rains.

Plant an agave as a dramatic specimen plant in a desert garden. Species range in size from 1 to 15 feet tall. All have sword-shaped, sharp-toothed leaves growing in a rosette. The leaf colors range, depending on the variety, from silvery blue and gray to bright green, as well as variegated green and yellow. Also known as the century plant, some species won't flower until they are at least 40 years old.

Create a quiltlike display in a cactus garden by mass planting, rather than dotting the landscape with single plants. When planning a cactus gar-den, capitalize on the wide choice of shapes, colors, and heights available from different varieties and species.

▶

Make a special corner in your garden for drought-tolerant plants using a simple design such as this one by Thomas Church for Longwood Gardens in Pennsylvania. The bench is surrounded by sedum "Autumn Joy," which has pretty pink flowers that dry to an ornamental bronze in the fall. Clumps of spiky yuccas behind and a bed of low-growing ornamental grass at the side provide interesting height and texture variation.

▲

A desert garden doesn't have to be a collection of cacti and succulents. Plant wildflowers native to dry regions of the world for a beautiful blooming desert garden. Here bright yellow African daisies *(Osteospermum)* flow informally around a patch of blue marguerites *Felicia.* Both are long-season bloomers native to South Africa.

▶

Producing flowers in many vibrant, glowing colors, Lampranthus belies its extreme drought tolerance and adaptability. Use various species to carpet bare ground with a colorful cover, especially on slopes where erosion control is important. Mass one color, or combine colors such as the yellow and orange shown here. The pink and magenta varieties also play well together.

▲
Gain access to land at the bottom of a steep cliff by zigzagging down the slope with paths and stairs. Here cacti and agaves decorate the way to the beach below. Cacti, which grow in rock crevices in the wild, are well suited to this precarious setting. Notice the cement bench molded into the hillside at the union of the two paths. The face of a cliff or hill can be a wonderful place for a seating area because the view is often spectacular.

▶
Build terraces to create level living space on a slope. Here the expanse of blank stucco wall is broken up with a planter built into the concave corner, brickwork on top, and a planting of azaleas in front. When the wisteria vine has completely covered the circular, spoked trellis on top, it will be a living shade umbrella.

▲
Traverse a slope with a natural stone path that can adapt to changes in level by becoming steps as well. Here dense plantings of thyme and sedum cover the hillside in a lush blend of greens and lavender. In addition to retaining the soil, the thyme adds a pleasant scent along the pathway.

Use the trunks of small trees to build a rustic railing along a steep woodland path. Here the white bark of birch trees makes a striking accent against the soft blue flowers of trailing blue phlox *(Phlox divaricata)*, which were planted as a ground cover.

Gertrude Jekyll, the famous English garden designer, popularized the idea of growing trailing roses to cover hillsides. She might have been impressed with this new "Meidiland" rose, which makes an ideal flowering ground cover. Meidiland roses are extremely hardy, disease-resistant, and need little or no pruning. The flowers begin in spring and continue into autumn, followed by bright-colored fruit.

A slope facing south and shaded by deciduous trees is a perfect location to plant early-flowering tulips. Choose from perennial varieties that come back with vigor each year, so that your tulip display doesn't diminish after just one season.

Plant drought-tolerant blooming plants—such as this collection of South African wildflowers mixed with aloes, ice plants, and sedums—to create a beautiful, low-maintenance tapestry of color and texture on a southern California hillside.

Mow a serpentine path through your meadow to make a special route from one point to another, such as a picnic area. This meadow is blooming with Indian paintbrush *(Castilleja indivisa)* and bluebonnets *(Lupinus texensis)*, both Texas natives.

To plant a meadow properly, it is best to first plow the land. If that's too much work, create islands of meadow flowers among native grasses by preparing patches of soil and seeding just those areas. Although the plants self-sow each year, a meadow mix will generally revert to just a few dominant plant varieties, so if you want to maintain a selection of flowers that bloom sequentially throughout the season, plan to reseed with meadow annuals each year.

Choose a meadow seed mix that will thrive in your region. The mix shown here includes poppies, which are a mainstay of most mixes; cornflowers; chrysanthemums; and rainbow daisies, an important ingredient in western mixes.

Sow a meadow as an attractive low-maintenance buffer between your property and a highway or busy road.

▼

In a desert rock garden, use terra-cotta pottery as accents to echo the color of the soil and shape of the surrounding stones. Pottery, in various shapes and colors, is a good decorating option for other rock garden settings as well.

◄

Create a garden of living "rocks" with a variety of lithops, native to South Africa. These tiny succulents break into two halves and bloom through the crevice. They need only infrequent watering in summer, none in the winter. Since they are frost-sensitive, these "pet rocks" can be planted outdoors only in warm regions, but since they are so small (most are less than an inch across), it's easy to grow an admirable collection inside.

▼

Instead of working to remove the stones from a rocky plot of land, turn the problem into an asset by planting among the stones. If necessary, add a bit of soil around the rocks to create planting niches. Here, pink phlox, yellow perennial alyssum, and white candytuft (Iberis sempervirens) tumble over and around the stones in beautiful abandon. Consider adding a stone or cement statue as an accent.

Even large cacti, such as these barrel species, can grow in small amounts of soil, making them ideal for rock gardens. This cactus rock garden is a raised garden room adjoining a tropical space planted with pale blue-flowering plumbago, pelargonium (geranium), and bougainvillea.

Use mass-planted chrysanthemums as an unexpected rock garden plant. Hardy perennial mums should be cut back each winter, after they bloom. They will return by summer and provide an attractive blue-green foliage cover until they flower again in autumn. Plant spring-blooming bulbs to add interest during the early months, before the mums sprout.

Large, unusual stones have the same effect in a garden as a piece of sculpture. Artist Walter Beck arranged these stones to create a naturalistic waterfall at his famous garden in Millbrook, New York, called Innisfree (see page 19). The water flows into a lower pool, where it is pumped back to the top of a slope through hidden pipes.

Extend the traditional concept of a rock garden by planting a stone seat with a shallow-rooted plant such as this yellow-blooming sedum.

▲
Cover a flat-roofed building with top soil, and grow shallow-rooted plants such as these succulents, which have been planted in a patchwork quilt pattern on a rooftop in Carmel, California. Be sure to check the weight-bearing ability of the roof before planting this kind of garden.

▶
Build a lath cover over part of a rooftop garden to screen the area from overlooking windows, provide shade, and support vining plants. Planters made of the same wood as the lath serve as partitions and edgings on this city rooftop deck.

▲
If you are building a house from scratch and the idea of a rooftop garden appeals to you, plan ahead with your architect and a landscape designer to make it possible. These terraced roofs in the village of Eze, France, were designed especially to support a garden, with large sunken planters provided for the trees and the roof pitched to drain off water.

Chop a hole in a rock with a pickax to create a planting container on a rocky coastline. If you find natural indentations or clefts among the boulders, simply fill them with soil and plant. Here petunias flourish in a bed hewn out of stone.

Line a path down to the beach with stepping stones, such as these "mill-stones," to help keep feet free from sand. Paperlike purple statice flowers (also known as sea lavender) on either side of this path are excellent as cut flowers, and will last for months even without water. Statice species grow wild along much of the California coast. Grow them as annuals in colder climates.

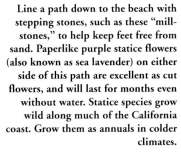

Consider using a beautiful, twisted piece of driftwood as a sculptural ornament in your seaside garden.

Build a wall as a windbreak in a coastal garden to make it possible to grow wind-sensitive plants such as vegetables. This wall protects a potato patch. It is low because the garden is on a cliff above the sea; at sea level, it would need to be taller. Use glass windbreaks that don't obliterate the view to protect beach-front seating areas from too much breeze.

Plant the coarse variety of ice plant, also known as sea fig or Hottentot fig, for a dependable seaside ground cover along the West Coast. *Carpobrotus chilensis*, with rosy purple flowers, is native from Oregon to Baja California. The yellow-flowering variety, *Carpobrotus edulis*, hails from South Africa. Both are unaffected by disease, insects, or smog, and thrive as easily in the shifting sands at the sea as in heavier clay soil. They are extremely drought-tolerant, although they need some irrigation to remain as lush and succulent as those shown here.

Toss quick-germinating flower seeds on a seaside bank to grow a dazzling ground cover for erosion control. Sprinkle straw over the seeds to keep them from blowing away, and water to keep them moist if rainfall isn't regular during the germination period.

Plant trees to protect a coastal garden from the wind, and use the microclimates created by your home to expand the variety of plants that will grow there. Here at Tor House in Carmel, California, the poet Robinson Jeffers wrote about his "planted forest . . . dark-leaved Australians or the coast cypress, haggard/ With storm-drift."

Plant impatiens for a continuous bright floral display in the shade throughout summer until the first frost. Although annual in cold climates, a bed like this, extended with pink petunias, will bloom year-round in frost-free areas. Hybridizing work in the world of impatiens now gives us a wide choice of plant forms from tall to short. The dwarf variety "Super Elfins" shown here will never grow leggy.

Related to dogwoods, the bunchberry *(Cornus canadensis)* is an excellent, low-growing ground cover for woodland areas in zones 2 to 7. Underused, perhaps because it is considered hard to establish, it will settle in happily and form a dense cover if planted in leaf mold. The flowers bloom in May or June. Clusters of bright, shiny red berries ripen in August and September, before the leaves yellow and die down.

Use tuberous begonias as a bedding plant to create an opulent, brilliantly colored shade display. Put each plant in a hole filled with planting mix. The flowers will face the same direction as the points of the leaves, so orient the leaf points toward the front of the bed. Water regularly, and feed monthly with a complete fertilizer. In hot, dry areas, mist the plants to keep them cool and humidify the air. Control mildew with benomyl.

Make the transition between sun and deep shade with plants that like a medium light level, such as astilbe, a feathery-flowered perennial that does best in partial shade. A hosta, which does well even in deep shade, is tucked under the the tree in this garden, while a blooming rose enjoys its place in the sun. In fact, most flowering shade plants need filtered sun to bloom properly.

▲
Trees near a lawn create an ever-changing pattern of dappled shadows. For a shady lawn to be successful, it's important to seed with a mixture that is predominantly fescue.

►
Prune lower branches to create a high canopy of shade for flowering plants, such as clivias, that need ample light, but no direct sun. Clivias, also known as Kaffir lilies due to their South African origins, are an important flowering shade plant for southern California and Florida. Here they are densely planted among boulders, a good situation because they flower better when root-bound.

▲
Flowers don't have to be the focus in a shade garden. Line a cool path or fill a shady bed with mass plantings of hostas. Find a good source for the plants; specialist perennial nurseries generally carry a wide variety. Have fun designing an attractive mix of leaf forms and colors.

Plant a large, spreading tree to create a cool microclimate in a hot garden. This California oak also shades the house, reducing cooling costs. Notice how the lower branches have been pruned to emphasize the tree's beautiful structure. The pruning also makes room for the fern planted underneath. Baby's tears *(Soleirolia)* is an excellent shady ground cover in temperate-climate gardens.

Put cascading varieties of shade-loving fuchsias in baskets and hang them under eaves, from porches and lath patio covers, or from tree branches to get a high spot of bountiful bloom throughout the summer. Pinch off the growing tips in early spring to encourage the plant to branch and produce more blooms. Fuchsias are heavy feeders; fertilize container plants often with a low-concentration of soluble fertilizer.

Use a bench to provide a welcoming shady haven from the sun. Here a trellis growing with vines helps create the shade, as well as screening this small garden from the road. The stone path through the informal planting of shade-tolerant hostas, impatiens, and ferns fits the relaxed, casual tone of the spot.

If you live in a cold climate, but have a desire to grow tropical plants, keep them in containers and bring them indoors for winter. On this Philadelphia rooftop, the ambitious owner grows tropical hibiscus; red-hot cattail or chenille plant *(Acalypha hispida)* with its furry red flower spikes; the pink-flowering vine mandevilla "Alice du Pont"; and, to its left, a coral vine *(Antigonon leptopus)*, which is just coming into bloom.

Truly a tropical plant, bananas like lots of heat, water, and feeding. Except in the most temperate regions, such as the southern California coast, they should be grown in a warm, protected spot or in a greenhouse or sunny window. To prevent the leaves from shredding, plant them out of the wind. Varieties range in size from huge, 20-foot high trees to dainty 4-foot plants.

Plant a tropical shade garden with palms, ferns, impatiens, and cymbidium orchids. Here, arching palm fronds create a tunnel along the side of a house, making what appears to be a miniature rain forest.

In a borderline tropical/subtropical region, such as much of San Diego County, California, use or create a microclimate to grow tropical plants. This sheltering wall collects and reflects the warmth from the sun, so it is excellent for plants that thrive on heat. Other possible places for tropical microclimates are enclosed patios and along the warm outside walls of your home.

▲

In a large lily pond, plant lilies in clumps to create islands. Here in Claude Monet's famous water garden in Giverny, France, note how the water around the lilies is left free of leaves to reflect surrounding scenes of sky above and willows drooping along the shore.

▼

Carefully arrange rocks to create a natural-looking woodland pond. The beautiful red leaves falling among the rocks and onto the water surface come from the shrub burning bush *(Euonymus alatus)*. The hardy green ferns, saxifrage, and mosses rimming the pool provide a striking contrast to the gray rocks and brilliantly colored foliage.

▼

Fish in a pond add color and movement to the scene. Perhaps the easiest pets to care for, fish can survive on submerged plants and mosslike algae that grows on the side of the pool. If you feed them fish food specially formulated for outdoor use, you will build a bond of friendship. Shown here are *koi*. If your winters are severe, consider goldfish.

Don't neglect the vast possibilities for leafy varieties in a water garden. Here lettucelike leaves of skunk cabbage, combined with umbrella-shaped mayapple leaves (to the right) and unfurling stalks of fiddlehead ferns, make an appealing woodland pondside scene. Another effective foliage combination is Japanese coltsfoot, with heart-shaped leaves as large as dinner plates, and iris spikes.

To rim a woodland pond, choose plants that blend with the environment. Pictured here are blue forget-me-nots, white phlox, rosy red primulas, and fiddlehead ferns. The yellow flag iris *(Iris pseudacorus)* is a good shore transition plant, growing happily in both boggy soil and directly in the water.

Interplant poolside plants to have blooms during different months. Here Livingstone daisies *(Dorotheanthus bellidiformis)*, an annual ice plant ground cover that blooms in dry, sunny areas, are mixed with tiger flowers *(Tigridia)*, which bloom after the ice plant blossoms have faded.

► Build a water garden into a courtyard to soften and cool the hardscape. The design of this Spanish-style water lily pool and fountain is excellent for hot climates, and especially appropriate in the Gulf states, Southwest, and coastal California, where Spanish influence is part of the history and architecture of the region.

◄ Geometric shapes arranged symmetrically give a water garden a more formal appearance. This shallow, square pool is rimmed with a border of hot-pink zinnias, framing the picture. Pink and yellow lantanas trained as standards add height to each corner of the frame as does the border of yellow blossoms behind. The two contrasting lantana colors unite the colors framing the pool, enlivening an otherwise static design.

◄ Use boulders to rim an informal water lily pool, and plant poolside greenery in the interstices. Here pebble beaches sloping into the water seem to break the shore of large stones. Notice that the slab of rock forming the bridge is different in shape and texture from the large, rounded boulders, but it blends well because it is the same color.

▶

Carpet a woodland glade with low-growing flowers such as these creamy white foamflowers *(Tiarella cordifolia)*, blue phlox *(Phlox divaricata)*, bright pink *Primula polyneura*, and native bleeding hearts, which all bloom in spring. The azaleas are a low-growing variety that won't dominate this delicate scene.

▶

Use exposed tree roots as natural planters for minor bulbs that remain near the surface, such as the blue glory-of-the-snow *(Chionodoxa)* shown here. Either scratch the bulbs into the earth or lay them on top and cover with extra soil.

▲

Plant a woodland garden with wildflowers. Here the white trillium, a native of the northeastern part of the country, nestles comfortably next to a dwarf yellow pieris on the right and yellow bellwort *(Uvularia)* in the center. Pieris grows especially well with rhododendrons since they are related and share growing requirements, such as acid soil.

▶

In a naturalized area, leave pine cones and needles on the ground. Cones have a fascinating form and texture and are a delightful feature in the garden, and fallen needles make an attractive brown, swirling pattern on the ground. The needles also create a soft, pine-scented cover that is a pleasure to walk on.

In the South, grow bald cypress *(Taxodium distichum)* in a wet, woodland garden. The knobs protruding from the water, called cypress knees, are special breathing roots produced by the trees. Growing in the water are yellow-flowered bladderwort *(Utricularia),* an insect-eating plant, while Atamasco lilies *(Zephyranthes atamasco)* bloom along the shore.

Make paths through your woods to create a pleasant stroll garden. If your property is small, design walkways so they double back on themselves, and use a dense plant to create screens between sections. Use a sharp bend in the path, where a walker will naturally slow down, as an opportunity to highlight a special plant—perhaps a small wildflower that otherwise would be easy to miss.

A grove of deciduous trees is an ideal spot for early spring–flowering plants that need sun, since they will bloom before the tree leaves have grown enough to block the light. Here snowflakes *(Leucojum aestivum)* and *Epimedium versicolor* "Neo-sulphureum" bloom profusely under the trees. Daffodils also do well in a woodland setting such as this.

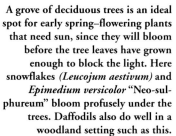

In frost-free regions, such as Florida and southern California, or in a protected conservatory, you can create a tropical jungle. In this small garden a background of philodendron vines and dragon trees *(dracaena)* disguises a high wall. Boulders with pockets of ferns and bromeliads provide height, orchids add color, and a rocky pool serves as a beautiful focal point.

Part of the magic of a woodland garden is that many horticultural miracles happen on their own, with little help from you, the gardener. Take a moment to notice the intimate beauty of the tiny mosses and ferns that thrive in a shady, damp woodland environment, and emulate these natural plantings in your own woodland garden.

Unique to the northeastern part of America, a springhouse is a delightful feature in woodland settings. Built over streams—or springs—in Colonial times, so the water flowing through could cool a storage area to preserve perishable foods, they are now appreciated for their structural charm and historical interest.

Native to Oregon and California, the West Coast redwoods *(Sequoia sempervirens)* are the tallest trees in the world. Despite their size, they make an admirable landscape plant. The trees grow from 3 to 5 feet a year and are hardy in most areas of the United States, so it is possible to establish a small grove of them in not too many years, as shown here at the Blake House in Kensington, California.

Color Theme Gardens

IN MOST GARDENS color has a more immediate visual and emotional impact than any other feature. A profusion of flowers in tones of red is stunning, uplifting, and cheery, while a garden of greens and blues can be soothing—a retreat for quiet contemplation.

Hiroshi Makita, a Japanese landscape designer whose work is well known in the Philadelphia area, describes gardening as an art form that uses flowers and plants as paint and the soil and sky as a canvas. Learning to employ color as an artist, using either new or traditional techniques, is important to any garden designer, and standard color theories are a good place to start.

Color Theory

Colors can be either warm (reds, yellows, and oranges) or cool (blues and greens). In most cases, warm colors seem to advance, appearing closer than they really are, while cool colors seem to recede. This effect can be used to create spatial illusions in a garden. For example, a marvelous way to make your garden feel larger is to plant cool tones of blue or purple at the far edges. If you plant warm-colored flowers in the distance, they will close the perceived space, making the garden appear smaller.

White flowers mixed with either warm or cool colors add definition, making the colors look brighter and cleaner. Gray foliage also accents the color of adjacent blooms. Next to gray, pastel tints are brighter and bold colors are even more intense. Paradoxically, grays also help moderate two colors that tend to fight.

Colors can be combined in many exciting ways. For a monochromatic garden, plant flowers in many tints or shades of a particular color, such as red, pink, and maroon, or variations on blue. This is the approach used to create some famous color theme gardens. Vita Sackville-West's well-known white garden at Sissinghurst in England (see page 175) uses silvery and gray foliage in addition to white flowers to create an all-white theme. In impressionist painter Claude Monet's memorable garden in Giverny, France, a bed of pink-blooming tree roses is underplanted with masses of pink geraniums and bordered with pink dianthus (see pages 46 and 174). The Italians are masters at creating green gardens that soften the lines of strong architectural lines and reduce glare to evoke a feeling of coolness.

A garden can be designed with analogous, or harmonious, colors—any three adjoining colors on the color spectrum, such as yellow, yellow-orange, and orange. Analogous colors are easier to work with than strictly monochromatic ones because there is a wider range of colors, and therefore plants, to choose from. Be sure, however, to keep your colors lively by using white or gray as an accent or by punctuating them with a splash of high-contrast color.

For an especially bold, electric look, plant a garden with complementary colors, such as yellow and violet, red and green, or orange and blue. Spring bulb gardens often vibrate with these dramatic color combinations. The Dutch love to see yellow daffodils forming a stunning contrast to deep blue grape hyacinths, a favorite planting theme in the gardens of Keukenhof, Holland. Heel-clicking ebullience is what's wanted after a long winter, which is why tulips, with their vibrant color range, are so popular with color enthusiasts. Generally, it is a good idea to use complementary color combinations as punctuation in a garden, to create a focal point or provide relief from possible monotony.

A polychromatic garden, with a random mix of flowers in

every color, is a less formal approach to garden color. The effect has the relaxed, casual look associated with a field of flowers or a mixed bouquet. If the colors are mostly bright, pure hues, the atmosphere can have a carnival feeling. There is an elemental appeal to a bold display of, say, zinnias blooming in every color available to that plant.

Color in Context

The quality of light, as well as the background or setting in which flowers are grown, will affect the appearance of colors. All-white gardens are especially beautiful when seen on misty mornings or overcast days, but tend to bleach out under the glare of cloudless summer skies, especially in an exposed midwestern or southern garden. Bright colors, such as pink, work well in shade because they reflect what light is available—it's surprising how many shades of pink the plant palette can provide. Pink flowers are also a lovely color contrast against a sweep of blue ocean or lake, while blue flowers are a popular seaside planting because they echo the color of the water. Yellow and

orange intensify in strong sunlight; they seem to grab the sunshine and hand it right back to you.

The translucent quality of leaves and petals is also important. Red and pastel-pink poppies can glow like Chinese lanterns viewed against a rising or setting sun. Combined with blue cornflowers in a meadow wildflower planting, the poppies create a spectacular display of contrasting color in strong sunlight. As the blue recedes with the setting sun, the backlit poppy petals shine brilliantly.

The structure of your garden and neighboring plants also affects how colors and designs are perceived. A garden generally looks best with a green or gray foliage framework. Without this unifying element, a basically good design may be ruined. In her book *Color in the Garden,* Penelope Hobhouse writes about a particular garden having an excellent overall design and structure, but not enough background green: "in almost every case a plant with colored leaves—in purple, glaucous, gold or variegated tones—has been used in preference to green . . . a sense of overall unity is missing. How much more effective it would have been to divide the garden into distinct color areas or themes, linked and framed by contrasting green shades."

Color Sources

While excessive use of colored foliage can lack harmony, in moderation it is an excellent source for color in your garden. In her white garden, Vita Sackville-West stretched the concept to include plants with gray and silver foliage such as lamb's ears *(Stachys byzantina),* beach wormwood, also known as dusty miller *(Artemisia stellerana),* and silver mullein *(Verbascum).*

Enhance a yellow garden with yellow-leafed plants such as hollies and hostas, which are variegated golden yellow and green, ornamental grasses with yellow blades, yellow-leafed privets or euonymus, and trees such as the Japanese maple "Aureum." The garden pictured on page 176 is an excellent example of combining foliage and flowers to extend a color theme.

In a blue garden, take advantage of the evergreen blue spruces, blue fescue, hosta varieties, agaves, and in warm climates, blue-leafed eucalyptus. Don't forget plants that bear decorative blue berries, such as *Mahonia aquifolium* and *Mahonia bealei.*

Lots of trees and shrubs have deep purple or red foliage. The Japanese red maple is a popular choice, but don't forget other possibilities such as barberry *(Berberis thunbergii),* *Bergenia cordifolia* "Purpurea," and pieris when the growth is young. Experiment with unusual red-leafed bedding plants such as *Iresine herbstii* "Brilliantissima," the red-veined Swiss chard called "Ruby Chard," and coral flower *(Heuchera americana).*

Architectural features, such as bridges, gazebos, benches, or even a house, are another source of color in the garden. Claude Monet painted his house pink with green shutters. The green, of course, is echoed throughout the garden in foliage, but he also painted his famous Japanese bridge and trellis the same striking green (see page 103), as well as the benches placed throughout the garden (page 101). He matched several flower beds to the pastel pink of the house (see pages 46 and 174).

The traditional Japanese moon bridge is painted bright orange-red. On page 103, a yellow bridge is used as a cheerful accent in the landscape and complements the yellow foliage of the trees beyond; and on page 176, a gazebo painted orange accentuates the bronze foliage of Japanese maples and an azalea's orange blossoms. There are times and places where a bold, confident splash of color is exactly right.

Designing for Color Interest

Depending on the size of your garden and your whim, you may want to devote one section to a specific color theme with permanent plantings of perennials and shrubs accented with annuals. Or, if you prefer variety, use annuals in a bed and change the colors to suit your mood each season or from year to year.

Designing a garden for color is not easy. Even Vita Sackville-West, who is considered one of England's premier garden designers, expressed anxiety about the success of her proposed white garden, although it is now considered one of the most beautiful gardens in Britain. So arm yourself with color knowledge, and then try out an idea and see how it works. With careful planning, and perhaps some trial and error, you can create a beautiful color theme garden.

▲

Dynamic because it is unusual, a blue garden has an irresistible, cool, peaceful feeling about it. Add a few splashes of pink and red, as shown here, to give vibrancy to the design. White flowers will intensify the sense of blue by giving it definition.

▶

The obvious choice for an all-green garden is a clever mix of foliage plants. For added interest, include plants that produce green flowers. Here the large green *Euphorbia wulfenii* blossoms enhance a corner of the garden. As an annual, the flowers last well when cut and are also good for drying. Other green-flowering plants include zinnia "Envy," Nicotiana "Limelight," and gladiolus "Green Woodpecker."

▲

Hostas are a treasure in a shade garden because of the remarkable variety of leaf forms and colors available in several hundred hybrids. Use them in a blue or green garden design to create a beautiful ground cover quilt by combining different kinds. In this small cluster alone are greens ranging from blue to yellow to dark green edged with creamy white.

Combine flower colors with the same care you would use to mix decorator colors in your home. In Claude Monet's garden in Giverny, France, massed pink tulips underplanted with red English daisies are a pleasing combination, which blends well with the farmhouse beyond. Flower colors can have a strong influence on people. Two years before he died, Monet said, " I perhaps owe having become a painter to flowers."

"Lord Baltimore" *(Hibiscus moscheutos)* has a hot crimson, iridescent coloring that adds vibrancy to this otherwise pale pink composition of "Rosy Future" zinnias and cleomes (spider flowers). Use a bold color from the same palette to add zing to a monochromatic color design.

Plant a sensational monochromatic garden by choosing different shades of pink from one type of plant such as these feathery astilbe, hardy perennials that grow best in partial shade. Their showy flowers are attractive even when dried brown in winter.

Use plants of varying heights in your color scheme as shown in this enchanting study in pink. Low-growing sweet William *(Dianthus barbatus)* in shades ranging from pale to shocking pink grow in front of a backdrop of tall pink and white Canterbury bells *(Campanula medium)*. In back, a deep pink rhododendron and tall pink and white foxgloves will soon be in full bloom. This combination of plants does particularly well in the cool climate of the Pacific Northwest.

Even a small bed of white-blooming plants can add a splash of exotic interest in your garden. Here the large white blossoms of hibiscus "Southern Belle" are a pleasing contrast to the smaller blooms of white-flowering zinnias, euphorbias, and cleomes.

Plant a white garden you can enjoy at night by the light of the moon. Perhaps the best-known white garden in the world is the one planted by Vita Sackville-West at Sissinghurst, her home in England. In early summer, white-blooming roses, calla lilies, poppies, and feverfew *(Chrysanthemum parthenium)*, combined with silver-leafed plants, create a garden that is spellbinding day or night.

Silver and gray plants add texture in a white garden, as well as creating a theme garden of their own. Here the tall silver mullein *(Verbascum)* curves protectively around the low lamb's ears *(Stachys byzantina)* and dusty miller *(Artemisia ludoviciana)* "Silver-King." Many of the silver plants do well in sandy, salty soil, making them ideal for seaside plantings.

Add a splash of blue in a white garden, such as these bluebells popping up among the white foamflowers *(Tiarella cordifolia)* and azaleas, as a cheery accent. The look is different from a completely white garden, but equally appealing.

We think of foliage being green, but actually it comes in a wide range of colors, depending on the plant. Use foliage as an unexpected source of color in a color theme garden. Here the yellow-leafed privet is a striking background to the tulips blooming in two shades of yellow. Behind the yellow garden is a composition of orange, with bronze Japanese maples, orange azaleas, and a gazebo painted bright orange to tie it all together.

Create a fascinating composition of varying textures expressed in only one color by planting a wide variety of flowers. Here the gladiolus, plumed celosia, American marigolds, tuberous dahlias, nasturtiums, and zinnias are all the same hue of yellow. The effect would have been completely different if the flowers had ranged from soft to bright yellow.

Plant a bed or border with flowers in colors next to each other on the color wheel, such as orange and yellow or blue and violet, for a color scheme that is stimulating as well as harmonious. Claude Monet, who preferred to paint outdoors, first planted a garden "so that there would be flowers to paint on rainy days." Here in his garden in Giverny he created a sunny, warm-colored border dominated by yellow loosestrife *(Lysimachia punctata)*, orange and yellow lilies, and orange and yellow pansies.

Seasonal Gardens

WHEN GARDEN EXPERTS from Europe and the Orient visit North America, they are struck by the significant seasonal differences, particularly in the northern states. Spring is greener and stimulates a more intense blooming of wildflowers than in either Europe or the Orient. Some of the woodland wildflowers will even break dormancy, sprout green leaves, flower, set seeds, and die—all before the deciduous trees are in full leaf. In many areas the entire season is cool and comfortable, allowing cool-season flowers such as pansies, calendulas, and snapdragons to bloom continuously.

North American summers, on the other hand, are generally hot and humid. Warm-season plants, such as hardy hibiscus, zinnias, cannas, and caladiums, bloom against a foliage canopy of dark greens. In vegetable gardens, cantaloupes, tomatoes, peppers, watermelons, and okra thrive on the long days and warm nights characteristic of most regions.

In autumn there is an incredible transformation in leaf colors. Nowhere else in the world is the beauty of autumn so pronounced as in the northern states of North America. Colors are especially intense in native trees such as maples, scarlet oaks, hickories, sassafras, liquidamber, tulip trees, and black tupelos—ranging from russet to buttercup yellow, lime-green, purple, and crimson. Though regions with no snow cover or sharp, prolonged freezing temperatures do not experience such a noticeable change in leaf colors, autumnal hues come in more subtle ways—with berries, for example. Where there *is* snow cover and freezing winter temperatures, it is difficult to get floral color during the winter months, but it's surprising how much color you can maintain with berry displays, colorful bark, and structures that can look exquisite covered with a mantle of snow.

Some gardens are designed especially to be viewed in one season, such as those with a spectacular display of spring flowers. People will travel miles to see a famous azalea garden or rose garden in full bloom. The Keukenhof flowering bulb garden in Holland attracts a million visitors each spring.

It is also exciting to observe the cycle of growth in a garden where the floral focus moves from one group of plants to another. Though harder to achieve, a garden designed to be enjoyed in every month, with something in bloom most of the year, is what most home gardeners prefer.

Planting for Year-Round Interest

There are two ways to maintain a succession of floral color in your garden all four seasons of the year. The first is to grow seasonal plants in separate beds, so that as one planting scheme fades, another comes into bloom. The more complex option is to try to orchestrate an all-seasons border that relies on annuals, flowering bulbs, perennials, and flowering shrubs to produce a parade of color. The flowering bulbs, perennials, and flowering shrubs will have short blooming periods (usually no more than 2 weeks of peak color), but a careful selection of annuals can provide "everlasting" color, so that even as the other plant groups come in and out of bloom, color is always sustained.

Planting spring-blooming bulbs will provide a backbone of color early in the year. Snowdrops and aconites will bloom even before the last snow falls in winter, as early as February, while some of the late-blooming tulips and daffodils will hold off until April or May. Choose a variety of early, midseason, and late bulbs to extend the display throughout the spring months.

Flowering shrubs and trees that bloom in spring complement spring bulbs beautifully. Azaleas, forsythia, flowering quince, and magnolias are ever popular, as are spiraea, flowering crab apples, and flowering cherries. In the western region of the country, consider such California natives as pink tree mallow (*Lavatera assurgentiflora*), California lilac (*Ceanothus thyrsiflorus*), and flannel bush (*Fremontodendron californicum*), which produce pretty flowers on an attractive shrubby plant.

For color in summer, concentrate on annuals and perennials. Most perennials bloom for a few weeks and then fade, while many annuals will keep on blooming until frost kills them. Arrange your perennials so that they bloom in an attractive progression and intermix them with annuals to provide variation in height, with tall background accents.

Let the harvest moon shine on New England asters, chrysanthemums, dahlias, helianthus, and pansies (a cool-weather flower that should continue to bloom until buried in snow). Hardy, perennial asters will grow back each year, making them an easy, satisfying plant to grow. Simply cut them back to the ground once they've finished blooming and consider dividing every 3 years. Some cushion-type chrysanthemums, on the other hand, especially those purchased from garden centers, may be too tender to survive a severe winter.

In regions with severe winters, concentrate on color from berries, decorative bark, and colored branches, such as the red-twig dogwood. A bare tree with a distinctive silhouette can be beautiful. Trees that have both an artistic tracery of branches and decorative bark include paper-bark maples and crape myrtle. Grow a few evergreens with pine cones (such as Norway spruce) to break the monotony of a bare winter landscape.

In the warm southern climates, plant sasanqua and japonica camellias for flowers throughout the winter, from November through March. The sasanquas will bloom first.

Spring

Before deciduous trees start to unfold their leaves, apply compost to flower beds and vegetable plots, and rake a granular fertilizer into the upper soil surface. After the soil has warmed, apply a decorative organic mulch to beds and borders.

By combining flowering bulbs, early-flowering perennials, and early-flowering shrubs, you can achieve a greater concentration of color in spring than any other time of year. Some of the best plants for spring flowers are azaleas, camellias, cherries, crabapples, daffodils, dogwoods, forsythia, irises, magnolias, mountain phlox, pansies, peonies, poppies, redbuds, rhododendrons, snapdragons, tulips, and wisteria.

Summer

Summer months can be hot and humid in North America. Watering is critical and booster applications of fertilizer may be necessary, especially for vegetable gardens and perennial beds. Small-space gardens can be watered with watering cans or hoses, but larger spaces are best watered with lawn sprinklers. If you live in a drought-prone region, invest in a drip-irrigation system, preferably one that can be buried.

Deadheading will keep flowering plants blooming longer. Deadheading involves pruning faded flowers so that the plant's energy is directed into stimulating more flower buds rather than into seed production. As flowering shrubs finish blooming, they can be pruned to maintain a compact shape.

Some colorful summer flowers include agapanthus, begonias, cockscombs, daylilies, garden lilies, geraniums, gladiolus, hollyhocks, hostas, hydrangeas, impatiens, marigolds, petunias, roses, rudbeckias, shasta daisies, water lilies, and zinnias.

Autumn

Many flowering annuals and perennials will continue flowering until a hard frost. Though a large number of trees and shrubs are noted for fall coloring, their colors vary considerably. To ensure the most satisfying fall colors, visit a tree farm and purchase those plants that display the best colors in your area.

Early autumn is a good time to seed a new lawn since there is less competition from annual weeds than in spring, allowing new grass to establish a dense weed-suffocating cover. Fall is also the best time to plant spring-flowering bulbs, such as tulips and daffodils. At the same time, feed naturalized bulb plantings with a high-phosporus fertilizer so they multiply freely.

Here are some flowers for autumn color: angel's trumpets, New England asters, coleus, cosmos, chrysanthemums, dahlias, helenium (sneezeweed), helianthus (sunflower), lantanas, monkshoods, nasturtiums, ornamental grasses, pansies, repeat bloom roses, Russian sage, and autumn-flowered sedums.

Winter

To escape the winter doldrums, many people in North America make an exodus to warmer climates, especially to southern Florida and the Southwest, where floral color is easily maintained year-round. But the truth is that many northern gardens can look spectacular in winter, particularly after a snowfall. Some snowfalls can be dangerous, however. If a strong wind springs up while branches are frozen, you can hear the sound of branches crashing to the ground. When a snowfall coats hedges and prize specimen shrubs, take a broom and sweep the branches clean to prevent the snow from freezing, avoiding damage to leaves and dormant flower buds. If not swept clear of snow, boxwood leaves especially will turn an ugly brown and take a long time to fill in with new foliage cover.

Color in winter is possible using the following flowering plants and shrubs with beautiful berry displays and colorful bark: aconites, adonis, camellias, Siberian dogwoods (bark), fire thorns (berries), hellebores, hollies (berries), dwarf irises, maples, pussy willows, skimmia (berries), snow crocuses, snowdrops, winterberries, winter hazels, and witch hazels.

▼

Get a head start on spring growth by planting flower, vegetable, and herb seeds indoors before the last frost. By the time the weather is warm enough to plant outdoors, you will have strong young seedlings. Before putting these tender plants in the garden, "harden-off" by setting them outside in a warm spot for a few hours a day to acclimate them to the new environment.

▶

Enjoy an early spring indoors with warm-climate winter-blooming flowers such as cyclamen and primrose, and flowering bulbs, such as amaryllis, *Iris reticulata*, and paperwhites. All will bloom during winter months if grown inside. Paperwhites will grow in a bowl filled with pebbles and water, and will bloom 3 to 4 weeks after planting. Plant a group for a Thanksgiving display and another batch for Christmas.

▲

Protect young plants from late frosts by covering them at night with over-turned peach baskets. It's an easy and very decorative solution. Ideally you should take the basket off as the day warms so the seedlings can benefit from the light, but if you forget one day, it will not harm the plants.

▲

Store your garden tools where they will keep dry and be easily accessible. Among the essential tools you need are spades, pruning shears and saws, a hand trowel, and a digging fork. Three kinds of shovels are useful: a wide one for shoveling lightweight material such as manure, peat, and leaf mold and two digging spades, one with a flat edge for edging and one pointed for deep digging.

In summer, go through your flower garden periodically and cut off the dead or dying flowers. In addition to keeping the garden more sightly, deadheading increases the vigor of many plants. Annuals, in particular, benefit from cutting, producing more flowers each time the old ones are removed. Cut lots of fresh blossoms to enjoy indoors as well.

As daffodil flowers die, nourishment flows back from the leaves into the bulbs, so it is important not to cut back their foliage until at least 6 weeks after flowering. To keep the garden looking tidy, tie up daffodil leaves with twine or rubber bands, and interplant with annuals that will grow to hide their fading leaves.

Keep varmints away from a strawberry patch, as shown here, or other vulnerable fruits and vegetables with a wire-covered cold frame. This split-rail fence has been covered with an unobtrusive wire netting as well to keep out rabbits and deer. Drape netting over fruit trees to save the fruit from hungry birds.

Instead of using commercially bought stakes, consider making a decorative support out of twigs. Notice how the side branches have been woven together at the top to create a dome. This English approach to staking is especially effective for vining annuals such as sweet peas and morning glories. The twigs look attractive while the young plants are gaining height, until eventually they are hidden by the covering vine.

Choose a simple garden ornament, such as this birdbath, as a centerpiece in a glade. In the autumn, the bowl of water will float the fallen leaves like little boats; it also serves as a miniature reflecting pool for the glorious russet colors. The cathedral-like atmosphere in this protected glade takes on a new dimension in autumn. The trunks of tall red oak and beech trees are more visible than in summer and look like gothic pillars reaching to the sky. Their yellow and gold leaves contrast with the evergreen shrubs that surround the glade. As the leaves carpet the grass, they unite the close and distant views.

Golden ginkgo leaves, like tiny fans, make a lacy pattern on this brick terrace. Wait a bit before you clean up fallen leaves to allow nature to create her own transient designs.

Design a spot in your garden to be a tableau of carefully balanced autumn colors, textures, and forms. Here the smooth, broad rhododendron leaves contrast beautifully with the spiky, blue-green foliage of holly and the pale and dark green needles of yew and hemlock. Their varying mounded, conical, and tall forms are accented by the straight, scaly trunk of the bare dogwood tree. The path of fallen dogwood leaves flows like a river around a bend, luring the eye and spirit to unknown mysteries beyond the planting.

▲

For a dramatic display of red-orange berries from late summer through winter (depending on the variety), plant pyracantha, also known as fire thorn. Different varieties of this flexible evergreen shrub can be grown upright, in small mounds, or as broadly sprawling forms that are ideal to espalier. Many types are hardy throughout the country.

▲

An arbor festooned with vines, such as the grapes pictured here, becomes a golden pathway in autumn. Other vines for autumn color include Virginia creeper and Boston ivy. The same effect can be obtained by planting vines to grow over a lath patio cover.

◄

A pond or pool is a lovely focal point in a garden at any time of year. Plant a tree for beautiful fall foliage near a pool, and enjoy the double sight of the tree reflected in the water and the colorful leaves floating in random patterns on the surface.

Fall-blooming mums are a diverse group, with blossoms ranging from less than 1 inch across to more than 6 inches in diameter, and flower forms including single, double, "pompons," "squills," and "spiders." Plant them in the ground or in pots for a final floral display before winter. In areas with harsh winters, choose cold-hardy breeds such as the Cheyenne series, which will return year after year.

The miniature pumpkins on the wheelbarrow are "Jack-be-Little," a recent introduction that is immensely popular for both cooking and decorating. Use them on your front porch, on windowsills, or outside in the garden as an easy way to add autumn color.

Ornamental grasses are an often-neglected source of fall interest and color in the garden. There are many species and varieties, each with distinct growth habits and forms. Create a living tapestry by planting a pleasing collection such as this grouping of miscanthus.

Design a perennial bed to be spectacular in autumn as well as spring and summer. This one has plenty of fall color interest with blooming canna lilies, Mexican and pineapple sage, blue salvia, plume poppies, and brightly colored clumps of low-growing mums.

Bright white snow accentuates the sculptural qualities of a finely pruned hedge. The deep recesses are darker, more noticeable, against the white, and the slanting angle of the sides more apparent. Even the curl at the tip of the low hedge bordering the path to the gate is more finely etched when covered with snow.

Blue *Iris reticulata* will push up through melting snow, providing a refreshing splash of color in February that lasts about 2 weeks. Aconites and snowdrops are two other determined bulbs that will brave snowfall to bloom. All three perform best in areas where they get winter chill.

A snow cover accentuates the structure of plants and objects. For an interesting winter garden, plant a variety of trees and shrubs that grow in fascinating shapes, such as the twisting branches of this Japanese maple *(Acer palmatum)*.

Bark on paths has an insulating effect, keeping them warmer than bare ground, so snow there melts faster. Other organic materials that have the same effect include licorice root, wood chips, and shredded leaves. With the paths relatively clear, the formal symmetrical design of these garden beds is highlighted by light snow cover.

Structures will add interest in a garden any time of year, but especially in deep winter. Here a gazebo with a sharply pitched conical roof is a focal point in an otherwise bare winter landscape. The gazebo's stone foundation matches the stone bridge, and its wooden surfaces are painted the same color as the shutters on the house, uniting it to both the natural surroundings and the nearby home.

Streams are a wonderful garden feature in winter because they remain alive and in motion except in the coldest freezes. In this garden, the carefully placed moss-covered rocks in the stream bed are particularly appreciated in winter when the snow masks other distinctions in the landscape. Their mounded forms add texture in an otherwise fairly smooth garden, and the green moss is a welcome relief from gray and white.

Witch hazels *(Hamamelis)* are prized for their year-round beauty. In winter, this cold-hardy plant produces a profusion of fragrant, frost-resistant flowers along its leafless branches. Witch hazel will grow in full or partial sun, doing best in well-drained, acidic soil. The final size of the plant depends on the variety. Chinese witch hazel, pictured here, grows as an upright, open shrub up to 12 feet wide and high.

Trees, woody shrubs, water, and boulders are the "bones" of a winter garden. When everything else has died, they remain as the basic skeleton. If the landscape is well designed, these bare forms are beautiful on their own. This monumental stone, covered in ivy, works as a garden feature, serving the same design purpose as a birdbath, sundial, or piece of sculpture.

Without the cover of leaves or blooms, you can see the beautiful blood-red stems of this red-barked dogwood *(Cornus alba)*. Dogwoods grown for winter stem color do best in full sun. Other trees that have distinctive bark for a winter garden are Scotch pine *(Pinus sylvestris)*, which is papery in texture, and hackberry *(Celtis)*, which is smooth and charcoal gray.

Bright red berries of American holly *(Ilex opaca)* add spice to a winter landscape. They also attract hungry birds, such as cardinals, which are like living Christmas ornaments—a joy to watch at any time of year.

Winter aconites *(Eranthis hyemalis)* are particularly striking when they are planted in drifts around trees. If they are grown in rich, fast-draining soil that has lots of humus, they will naturalize easily, returning each winter with ever more abundant golden flowers. The blooms last up to 2 months from late winter to early spring.

▲
Conifers come in a wide choice of color, size, shape, and texture and make an excellent choice to provide structure as well as perpetual green to the garden. Mix them carefully to create a tableau that blends as a beautiful composition but also showcases their individual characteristics. Dwarf varieties are valuable to create the same effect on a smaller scale.

▲
In tropical and subtropical regions, the winter months can be a time of profuse bloom, if the right plants are chosen. The cymbidiums shown here flower from December until May, depending on the variety, and can be grown outdoors in zone 10. Camellias and azaleas also bloom in midwinter, and flowers such as geraniums, impatiens, and euphorbias continue to produce color year-round.

◀
Whether dusted with snow or not, ornamental grasses are a big asset in a winter garden. There is a wide selection of hardy perennial varieties to choose from. Many retain their color throughout winter, such as the fountain grasses (center), maiden grass (right), and ribbon grass (below), while others bleach to an attractive beige like the tall stalks of giant miscanthus in the background.